Engaging Reluctant Readers Through Foreign Films

Kerry P. Holmes

With
izabeth L. Glenn Stuart and Mary H. Warner
Illustrator, Mike Jones

ScarecrowEducation
Lanham, Maryland • Toronto • Oxford
2005

Published in the United States of America
by ScarecrowEducation
An imprint of The Rowman & Littlefield Publishing Group, Inc.
4501 Forbes Boulevard, Suite 200, Lanham, Maryland 20706
www.scarecroweducation.com

PO Box 317
Oxford
OX2 9RU, UK

British Library Cataloguing in Publication Information Available

Library of Congress Cataloging-in-Publication Data

Holmes, Kerry P.
Engaging reluctant readers through foreign films / Kerry P. Holmes, with Elizabeth L. Glenn Stuart and Mary H. Warner.
p. cm.
Includes bibliographical references and index.
ISBN 1-57886-206-X (pbk. : alk. paper)
1. Reading (Secondary) 2. Reading—Remedial teaching. 3. Foreign films—Study and teaching (Secondary) I. Stuart, Elizabeth L. Glenn. II. Warner, Mary H. III. Title.

LB1632.H67 2005
428.4'071'2—dc22

2004024011

™ The paper used in this publication meets the minimum requirements of American National Standard for Information Sciences—Permanence of Paper for Printed Library Materials, ANSI/NISO Z39.48-1992.
Manufactured in the United States of America.

To my husband, Stacy, for his unending support and interest.
I especially want to thank him for his patience,
watching hours upon hours of foreign films, good and bad,
to help me find the perfect ones for this book.

Contents

Acknowledgments

I wish to thank a great many people who provided time, energy, resources, and ideas to make this book possible including public school teachers, dedicated university students, professors, and people within the community who enabled me to acquire the necessary resources to develop this book. I would like to thank the following people specifically:

Mary Warner, an art history honor student who assisted me with the writing of the film guides. Her insights into the setting, characters, and plot add depth and a thoughtful dimension to the film guides. She is a member of Phi Beta Kappa.

Elizabeth Glenn Stuart, a secondary education honor student who assisted me with the selection of films for this book. She wrote preliminary film guides, supplying many perceptive ideas for questions and activities. She meticulously correlated her ideas with the national standards for social studies and the English language arts. She is a member of Phi Beta Kappa.

As Seen on TV, the local video store that allowed me to keep the movies I rented for an indefinite time without penalty.

Cheryl Grisham, a social studies teacher at Senatobia Junior High School in Senatobia, Mississippi, provided some of the ideas for activities in this book. She shared important views on preadolescent and adolescent students and how they learn.

Leanne Young, a reading teacher at Senatobia Junior High School in Senatobia, Mississippi, loaned me books on remedial reading and provided excellent information about the needs of her students and ways to motivate them to read.

Both Ms. Grisham's and Ms. Young's enthusiasm, dedication to their students, and love of teaching are reasons Senatobia Junior High School, Senatobia, Mississippi, has earned the highest state accreditation rating.

Allison Movitz, a national board certified secondary English teacher at Bruce High School, Bruce, Mississippi, "teacher proofed" the activities in this book. She offered suggestions for activities based on her classroom experiences and opened her classroom to me so I could interact with high school students while writing this book.

The Mississippi Writing Project exposed me to other writers and provided a forum for exchanging research and writing ideas with K–12 classroom teachers.

Dr. Fannye Love, chair of the Department of Curriculum and Instruction, for her interest, support, and belief in my work.

Dr. Tim Letzring, an associate professor of leadership and counselor education at the University of Mississippi. He is also an attorney at law. He provided many resources concerning the use of copyrighted materials for education.

Mike Jones, illustrator for Patriot Greeting Card Company and whose cartoon, *Ricky's Tour*, runs regularly in the *Stars and Stripes* newspaper, I thank for sharing his artistic talents by providing the illustrations for this book.

The National Council of Teachers of English and the National Council for the Social Studies for granting permission to reprint the national standards.

Publish America for granting permission to reprint an excerpt from *Twelve Paper Cows* by John V. Holmes.

Chapter One

Introduction

It was Saturday night, and I was prepared to spend a relaxing evening watching a highly recommended foreign film with my husband. The movie, *East/West*, was a French film with English subtitles. This was to be a time when I intended to put all thoughts of school aside and treat myself to a "night out." At first I found reading the subtitles onerous. "I just want to be entertained without working at it," I complained. However, as the movie continued, I found myself being swept up in the plot and realized that I wanted to pay attention; I wanted to read the subtitles. Even when I missed a few words I was still able to follow the plot because the emotion of the words supplied by the actresses and actors in their native tongue, along with their actions, provided meaning. I found that reading became less of a burden as I became interested in the plot; at times I even forgot that I was reading to make sense of the plot.

About midway through the film my thoughts drifted to the students in the middle school where I was supervising student teachers. My student teachers were very concerned about students who were unable to read, even at a functional level. Because reading came hard for these students, they avoided it. Could foreign films with English subtitles be a way to engage older students in reading? This question has led to the development of a book on using foreign films with English subtitles for students in middle, junior, and secondary grades.

My student teachers were justified in their concerns about the reading skills of their students. The National Assessment of Educational Programs 2003 reading report card reports that 26% of eighth-grade students scored below the basic level in reading (NAEP 2003). This means that these students have not demonstrated even a partial mastery of the fundamental prerequisite knowledge and skills necessary for reading. Unless steps are taken, one out of every four of our nation's students will likely go through life avoiding books and other forms of written text. They will compensate for their poor reading skills by taking easier classes, dropping out of school, and ending up in low-level jobs requiring little reading. A primary goal of education is to prepare students to be productive in their society. Today, being productive is dependent on written communication; students must acquire literacy skills that will put the world literally at their fingertips.

This book is intended to reach those students in grades 6–12 who demonstrate a pronounced deficit in reading skills yet at the same time engage the more proficient readers with interesting text and story lines. With the realization that it is an uphill battle to focus students on something that promotes feelings of frustration and failure, this book offers a novel way to capture the students' interest and stimulate their imagination.

Through the use of selected foreign films with English subtitles, students will become engaged in a sensory approach to reading. While viewing a film with subtitles, students use sight and sound simultaneously as they *read* the text accompanying the action and *hear* the spoken emotion of the words they are reading. During the process of reading, the characters, setting, and plot are brought to life, creating a context for learning.

Brain research on learning and its applications to classroom practice have shown that learning new knowledge and skills becomes more lasting when they are presented in a context understood by the student (Wolfe, 2001). When learning and reinforcing new vocabulary words, the meaning becomes much clearer and more easily learned when the words are used in context.

Sousa (2001) states that the brain is a "novelty seeker" (p. 5). The brain is stimulated by novel, unexpected events. Written text, supported with moving pictures and music, creates a novel context that facilitates students' efforts at reading.

We are all attracted to movement. Try teaching a lesson when people are walking past the door; students, even interested students, will focus on the movement. The detection of movement is an innate trait necessary for survival. If students are predictably attracted to movement, let's add movement to our reading lessons. Foreign films with English subtitles do this beautifully. Written text accompanied by movement may help students who have difficulty maintaining their focus when reading a book. Any movement beyond the book is bound to cause a disruption for a reader who is just partially engaged with text. Movement from the film serves to attract rather than detract students' interest and attention. Furthermore, movement on the screen supports the meaning of the text.

Students may feel overwhelmed when faced with long pages of text. The text in subtitles comes in brief spurts, often one or two short sentences at a time. Reading text from a book is limited to small black words on a white page, sometimes supported by still pictures or graphics. When watching foreign films with English subtitles, students are engaged simultaneously with three of the language arts areas: reading, listening, and viewing. Comprehension is enhanced when students engage multiple senses during reading. Reading comprehension and vocabulary development are supported through students' interest in the action and pictures that accompany written text.

Because foreign films come in many genres, including drama, crime, and historical fiction, teachers can match the film to the interests of the students. Students read at a faster rate and at a higher reading level when they are interested in what they are reading (Anderson, 1984). Furthermore, we know that learning is more likely to be remembered when attached to an emotional response (Sousa, 2001). Foreign films can involve students emotionally with the lives and cultures of people around the world.

When viewing foreign films, students enter the homes and workplaces of people from other countries. Once exposed to cultural differences, students are equipped to make comparisons between their lives and the lives of people around the world. Abstract similarities and differences between people and places become real, based on the vibrant visualizations provided by award-winning filmmakers. When students become a part of another person's world, they acquire knowledge and insights necessary for developing an appreciation and sensitivity for cultures and customs different from their own. The use of foreign films with subtitles for classroom instruction provides a way to promote multiculturalism and the integration of reading with history, current events, and social issues.

All films described in this book have been carefully screened according to the following criteria:

- Educational worth based on the national standards for the English language arts and social studies
- Interest of the plot to the students
- Suitable language and violence levels
- Lack of sexually explicit scenes, including nudity
- Technical aspects, including the speed of words as they appear in the subtitles and the general readability and quality of the printed text

Though little has been written about the effectiveness of using foreign films with English subtitles to promote reading skills for students in grades 6–12, some success at the college level has been reported. Hoffman (1993) reported that college students in a developmental reading program in Texas showed marked improvement in reading speed. In another study, Meigs and McCreary (1991/1992) found that foreign films with English subtitles motivated their students to want to read.

An empirical observation of students in Allison Movitz's eighth-grade reading class at Bruce High School in Bruce, Mississippi, showed her students were motivated to read when shown *Life Is Beautiful*, an Italian film. *Life Is Beautiful* is the story of one family's fight for survival in a German concentration camp during World War II. After using *Life Is Beautiful* to support an integrated reading and social studies unit on the Holocaust, Ms. Movitz shared the following information about her class:

1. The students thought it would be boring to read the subtitles, but instead they said it was fun.
2. During the film, the students stayed on task, watching with rapt attention.
3. The students did not want to stop watching the film at the end of the class period and asked when they could see it again. In fact, they begged to see more of the film. (Because of a 47-minute class period, students watched the film in 20-minute increments.)
4. It was clear that the students were reading the subtitles because they reacted to ongoing aspects of the film. For example they groaned when the little boy said he wanted to see his mommy, and they laughed at humorous situations where the humor was conveyed only through the subtitles.
5. *Life Is Beautiful* was an excellent way to begin a reading unit on the Holocaust. Because of the pictures and strong story line, the students became emotionally involved.

Before you use a foreign film with English subtitles with your class, be sure to preview it for content, interest, and overall suitability for the students you teach. Get out the popcorn and be prepared to spend a pleasant evening preparing for your class!

REFERENCES

Anderson, R. C. (1984). *Interestingness of children's reading material.* ERIC Report No. ED 248 487. Washington, DC: National Institute of Education.

Hoffman, J. (1993). Read a good movie lately? Using foreign films in reading. *Reading Today, 11*(3), 29.

Meigs, C., & McCreary, R. (1991/1992). Foreign films: An international approach to enhance college reading. *Journal of Reading*, *35*(4), 306–310.

NAEP. (2003). "Reading: The nation's report card," at nces.ed.gov/nationsreport card/reading (accessed May 27, 2004).

Sousa, D. A. (2001). *How the brain learns.* Thousand Oaks, CA: Corwin Press.

Wolfe, P. (2001). *Brain matters: Translating research into classroom practice.* Alexandria, VA: Association for Supervision and Curriculum Development.

Chapter Two

Connecting Foreign Films With English Subtitles to National Standards for Language Arts and Social Studies

In an era where teachers are increasingly asked to teach more subjects at a deeper level, the integration of social studies with language arts provides a meaningful way to connect skills from these disciplines. Foreign films enable teachers to integrate their curriculum while extending students' understanding of various countries and their people. Foreign films provide a connection between the students and their world.

A foreign film with English subtitles is easily aligned with the national standards for English language arts and social studies. These content areas are naturally integrated with one another within the story line of the film. Teachers can plan their lessons by consulting the standards and relating them to the concepts they wish to emphasize from the plot of the film. By identifying concepts dramatized by the film and connecting them to the standards, teachers will have created authentic and purposeful opportunities for students to read, solve problems, and examine critical issues within a real-life context.

STANDARDS FOR THE ENGLISH LANGUAGE ARTS

In 1996 the International Reading Association and the National Council of Teachers of English published *Standards for the English Language Arts*. The purpose of the standards is to advocate teaching and learning in the six areas of language arts: reading, writing, speaking, listening, viewing, and visual representing. The standards, written by educators, are intended to serve as guidelines for curriculum planning and teaching English in grades K–12.

To illustrate how viewing foreign films with English subtitles immerses students in reading and the other areas of the language arts, each standard (NCTE, 1996) is listed here, followed by a brief description of the relationship of the standard to the use of foreign films in the classroom.

1. *Students read a wide range of print and nonprint texts to build an understanding of texts, of themselves, and of the cultures of the United States and the world; to acquire new information; to respond to the needs and demands of society and the workplace; and for personal fulfillment. Among these texts are fiction and nonfiction, classic and contemporary works.* Foreign films with English subtitles enable stu-

dents to read and interpret a "wide range of print and nonprint." Foreign films provide a multicultural glimpse into the lives and settings of people from around the world. Students learn about various cultures by reading, viewing, and listening to the sounds of human experience.

2. *Students read a wide range of literature from many periods in many genres to build an understanding of the many dimensions (e.g., philosophical, ethical, aesthetic) of human experience.* Foreign films come from many countries and represent slices of life from many periods of time. Engagement with foreign films helps students gain insights into the universal emotional nature of humans. Moral dilemmas and conflicts, at the heart of the plots, provide graphic and dramatic opportunities for students to make inferences based on the perspective of their experiences. Through the story line of the film, students can reflect on the moral consequences of actions.
3. *Students apply a wide range of strategies to comprehend, interpret, evaluate, and appreciate texts. They draw on their prior experience, their interactions with other readers and writers, their knowledge of word meaning and of other texts, their word identification strategies, and their understanding of textual features (e.g., sound-letter correspondence, sentence structure, context, graphics).* Students will "apply a wide range of strategies to comprehend, interpret, evaluate, and appreciate" the story expressed through the subtitles. The visual portrayal of the story line enables students to identify with the characters in the film. Students can use the tone and pitch of speech along with the actions of the characters to create meaning from the written text. The context of the story provides another powerful way for students to extract meaning from the written text. Foreign films portray a variety of human situations, providing numerous opportunities for students to question and refine their values and beliefs.
4. *Students adjust their use of spoken, written, and visual language (e.g., conventions, style, vocabulary) to communicate effectively with a variety of audiences and for different purposes.* By viewing foreign films and reading English translations, students have the opportunity to see, hear, and read different ways people communicate with each other in different situations. Interpretations and translations of colloquial expressions are interesting to compare and contrast with today's language

conventions. Students, by reading a broad range of dialogue, experience the social impact of spoken language.

5. *Students employ a wide range of strategies as they write and use different writing process elements appropriately to communicate with different audiences for a variety of purposes.* Because reading and writing are connected, students viewing foreign films not only gain a greater understanding of ways writers convey meaning and emotion through dialogue but can also use elements of the plot as a basis for their own writing. Through viewing foreign films, students expand their knowledge of the world and gain insights into human emotions, which stimulate reflective thinking necessary for writing.
6. *Students apply knowledge of language structure, language conventions (e.g., spelling and punctuation), media techniques, figurative language, and genre to create, critique, and discuss print and nonprint texts.* Written English translations of foreign films provide students a variety of language conventions, including spelling and figurative language. When reading the translation of a foreign film, students' reading is supported by music and the characters' body language, powerful vehicles for conveying meaning. Reading is also aided by the predictable text structure of the dialogue.
7. *Students conduct research on issues and interests by generating ideas and questions, and by posing problems. They gather, evaluate, and synthesize data from a variety of sources (e.g., print and nonprint texts, artifacts, people) to communicate their discoveries in ways that suit their purpose and audience.* Foreign films with English subtitles represent an excellent source for researching and gathering data on a multitude of cultures. Students are treated to an in-depth view of people's lives in different times and places, which they can use to clarify concepts and ideas. Viewing and reading foreign films provide opportunities for students to gain an appreciation of the use of language as a powerful communication tool.
8. *Students use a variety of technological and informational resources (e.g., libraries, databases, computer networks, video) to gather and synthesize information and to create and communicate knowledge.* Through the use of subtitled films, students gain another way to engage with text. Text is supported by sights and sounds, creating a multisensory context for reading. Students will use a variety of technological

and informational sources to complete activities based on the cultures, geographical areas, historical events, and biographies from the films.

9. *Students develop an understanding of and respect for diversity in language use, patterns, and dialects across cultures, ethnic groups, geographic regions, and social roles.* Foreign films offer students continual opportunities to hear a variety of language patterns and dialects. Through this immersion in other languages, students get the chance to gain a greater respect and awareness for the diversity of languages used around the world. Students view universal human aspects—including the physical, emotional, and social needs of people—and make connections between their own lives and the lives of people around the world. Armed with new insights from the films, students may move beyond suspicion or passive acceptance of people different from themselves to an enthusiastic appreciation of cultural differences.
10. *Students whose first language is not English make use of their first language to develop competency in the English language arts and to develop understanding of content across the curriculum.* By matching students whose first language is not English with a film produced in their country, they are exposed simultaneously to written English and the spoken words of their native tongue. They have the advantages of hearing and viewing the delivery of communication in their native language supported by a corresponding written English translation.
11. *Students participate as knowledgeable, reflective, creative, and critical members of a variety of literacy communities.* Students are exposed to different genres available in foreign films, giving them many opportunities to compare their communities, lives, and cultural mores with those depicted in foreign films. Using the film's story as a context for discussion, students have the opportunity to explore and formulate new ideas with others who share a similar or common heritage.
12. *Students use spoken, written, and visual language to accomplish their own purposes (e.g., for learning, enjoyment, persuasion, and the exchange of information).* Foreign films afford students opportunities to use written and visual language to increase reading fluency, vocabulary development, and comprehension. Reading and viewing, used to get meaning from the plot of a film, is purposeful. Students who read for a purpose should begin to experience enjoyment, a critical step for becoming lifelong readers and thinkers.

TEN THEMES OF THE SOCIAL STUDIES STANDARDS

Curriculum standards for social studies were developed by the National Council for the Social Studies in 1994 to provide a curriculum framework for teachers in grades K–12. Teachers are encouraged to use the curriculum standards for social studies when planning their curriculum and designing their instruction. Social studies standards are organized around 10 interrelated themes based on the social sciences and related disciplines, including history, geography, civics, and economics.

The 10 social studies themes (NCSS, 2002) are presented here, with an accompanying description of the ways foreign films with English subtitles can be used as a vehicle for planning integrated social studies/language arts lessons.

I. *Culture. The study of culture prepares students to ask and answer questions such as the following: What are the common characteristics of different cultures? How do belief systems, such as religion or political ideals, influence other parts of the culture? How does the culture change to accommodate different ideas and beliefs? What does language tell us about the culture? In schools, this theme typically appears in units and courses dealing with geography, history, sociology, and anthropology, as well as multicultural topics across the curriculum.* Culture is chronicled in every foreign film to varying degrees. Events reflect the cultural mores of different times and places, providing a striking contrast to the students' lives today. By being drawn into a slice of life, students receive many opportunities to view cultural differences through the lives of the characters, thus developing a keener understanding of the social customs of the times. Furthermore, the commonality of the human condition is seen dramatically across language and cultural barriers.

II. *Time, Continuity, and Change. Human beings seek to understand their historical roots and to locate themselves in time. Knowing how to read and reconstruct the past allows one to develop a historical perspective and to answer questions such as the following: Who am I? What happened in the past? How am I connected to those in the past? How has the world changed and how might it change in the future? Why does our personal sense of relatedness to the past change?*

This theme typically appears in courses in history and others that draw upon historical knowledge and habits. People and their environments change over time; foreign films graphically depict these changes. By reliving the past through events in the film, students build images and knowledge that serve as a foundation for viewing events in their lives that change or remain constant with time.

III. *People, Places, and Environments. The study of people, places, and human-environment interactions assists students as they create their spatial views and geographic perspectives of the world beyond their personal locations. Students need the knowledge, skills, and understanding to ask and answer questions such as the following: Where are things located? Why are they located where they are? What do we mean by "region"? How do landforms change? What implications do these changes have for people? In schools, this theme typically appears in units and courses dealing with area studies and geography.* Students can explore the geographical locations of countries, major cities, historical sites, and ancient lands. They can make comparisons between the bodies of water and landforms seen in the film to the bodies of water and landforms found in their area. Foreign films help students look beyond their own world to see how water and landforms affect the development of civilized areas and the overall quality of human life.

IV. *Individual Development and Identity. Personal identity is shaped by one's culture, by groups, and by institutional influences. Students should consider such questions as the following: How do people learn? Why do people behave as they do? What influences how people learn, perceive, and grow? How do people meet their basic needs in a variety of contexts? How do individuals develop from youth to adulthood? In schools, this theme typically appears in units and courses dealing with psychology and anthropology.* Preadolescent and adolescent students are constantly making comparisons with and seeking approval of their peers. Peer influence is the major socializing agent of preadolescent and adolescent students. Students may be surprised and enlightened to learn that human nature and emotions are remarkably the same across times and places. Foreign films enable students to be drawn into the lives of others. Through these experiences, they gain insights about their own personal development and identity.

V. *Individuals, Groups, and Institutions. Institutions such as schools, churches, families, government agencies, and the courts play an integral role in people's lives. It is important that students learn how institutions are formed, what controls and influences them, how they influence individuals and culture, and how they are maintained or changed. Students may address questions such as the following: What is the role of institutions in this and other societies? How am I influenced by institutions? How do institutions change? What is my role in institutional change? In schools, this theme typically appears in units and courses dealing with sociology, anthropology, psychology, political science, and history.* Students may have a difficult time seeing how institutions impact their lives. Foreign films bring the institutions of school, church, family, government, and the judicial system to life. Meaningful connections between institutions and the lives of people are easily recognized and understood when seen within the context of the plot. In some of the films, students will gain an appreciation for institutions when they see people trying to live normal lives in anarchy or dictatorship, with no institutionalized support or defense from hardships and enemies.

VI. *Power, Authority, and Governance. Understanding the historical development of structures of power, authority, and governance and their evolving functions in contemporary U.S. society and other parts of the world is essential for developing civic competence. In exploring this theme, students confront questions such as the following: What is power? What forms does it take? Who holds it? How is it gained, used, and justified? What is legitimate authority? How are governments created, structured, maintained, and changed? How can individual rights be protected within the context of majority rule? In schools, this theme typically appears in units and courses dealing with government, politics, political science, history, law, and other social sciences.* Power and authority are often a cause of resentment for preadolescent and adolescent students. By viewing films with examples of power and authority, students receive the opportunity to see and feel the good and evil manifestations. Students will gain insights about power and authority that can help them make critical decisions about people and agencies they trust and support.

VII. *Production, Distribution, and Consumption. Because people have wants that often exceed the resources available to them, a variety of ways have evolved to answer questions such as the following: What is to be produced? How is production to be organized? How are goods and services to be distributed? What is the most effective allocation of the factors of production (land, labor, capital, and management)? In schools, this theme typically appears in units and courses dealing with economic concepts and issues.* Wars and revolutions have occurred based on disagreements on how to answer the four questions just presented. Watching the characters in other countries grapple with these ageless questions is broadening and encourages introspection into one's own views. Because most American students have grown up in a culture where goods and services are plentiful, many students may not have confronted life-threatening issues related to a lack of the production and distribution of goods and services, nor have they had to consider the consequences of waste. Many foreign films deal with tragedy that results when goods and services are not available.

VIII. *Science, Technology, and Society. Modern life as we know it would be impossible without technology and the science that supports it. But technology brings with it many questions: Is new technology always better than old? What can we learn from the past about how new technologies result in broader social change, some of which is unanticipated? How can we cope with the ever-increasing pace of change? How can we manage technology so that the greatest number of people benefit from it? How can we preserve our fundamental values and beliefs in the midst of technological change? This theme draws upon the natural and physical sciences, social sciences, and the humanities and appears in a variety of social studies courses, including history, geography, economics, civics, and government.* Preadolescent and adolescent students have grown up with technology that was virtually nonexistent to their parents. It is difficult to many students to realize that there once was a world without computers and cellular telephones. By viewing foreign films, these students can see how the world operated without the technological advances so common today. They will be able to make comparisons between their lives today and the lives of people living in an era without the benefit of today's technology.

IX. *Global Connections. The realities of global interdependence require understanding the increasingly important and diverse global connections among world societies and the frequent tension between national interests and global priorities. Students will need to be able to address such international issues as health care, the environment, human rights, economic competition and interdependence, age-old ethnic enmities, and political and military alliances. This theme typically appears in units or courses dealing with geography, culture, and economics, but may also draw upon the natural and physical sciences and the humanities.* The view that America is a nation protected by the great oceans was shattered on September 11, 2001. The term "shrinking world" took on new and terrible dimensions. International issues have become American issues. Students must gain a historical perspective on the ways America is connected to the world order. Foreign films offer perspectives and insights that have shaped many of today's policies.

X. *Civic Ideals and Practices. An understanding of civic ideals and practices of citizenship is critical to full participation in society and is a central purpose of the social studies. Students confront such questions as: What is civic participation and how can I be involved? How has the meaning of citizenship evolved? What is the balance between rights and responsibilities? What is the role of the citizen in the community and the nation, and as a member of the world community? How can I make a positive difference?* Through viewing foreign films, students can see instances of civic participation in other cultures. Civic participation runs from extreme passivity to mob rule, thus it is apparent that it creates both beneficial and adverse effects. Through events in the films, students will gain an appreciation for the complexity of human action.

REFERENCES

NCSS. (2002). *Expectations of excellence: Curriculum standards for social studies* (5th ed.). Silver Spring, MD: National Council for the Social Studies.

NCTE. (1996). *Standards for the English language arts.* Urbana, IL: National Council of Teachers of English.

Chapter Three

Vocabulary Instruction

This chapter provides numerous and varied ways for students to use and apply words from the subtitles of the films. The wisdom of one junior high remedial reading teacher, "You can't teach struggling students in the standard way; you'll lose them," captures the intent of this chapter (Leanne Young, Senatobia Junior High School, Senatobia, Mississippi). Activities in this chapter provide nonstandard yet academically sound ways to teach vocabulary.

Studies indicate that struggling readers benefit from a planned, systematic approach to vocabulary learning. Allen (1999) quotes Baker, Simmons, and Kameenui, researchers in reading instruction, to illustrate the need for systematic instruction for at-risk students. "Students with poor vocabularies, including diverse learners, need strong and systematic educational support to become successful and independent word learners" (p. 10). Many students may need to encounter a new word 10 to 15 times before the word is learned and retained. Time used for vocabulary instruction is well spent because of the integral connection between vocabulary acquisition and reading comprehension.

Teacher modeling is a powerful way to support students as they learn new material (Holmes, 2003). Show the students steps they can take to learn and understand words; reveal your thinking as you tackle new words and strive to make sense of them. This is where you can show your students how you make connections between new words and your experiences. Model the curiosity you feel as you encounter an unknown word, and describe the strategies you use to make sense of the word. It is important to augment instruction with objects and pictures students can use to build experiences with unknown concepts and the words that describe them. It is hard for students to grasp the meaning of new words if they are unfamiliar with the underlying concepts.

Once students gain a basic knowledge of words, it is important to provide opportunities for them to use their newly learned words in a variety of ways. One of the best ways for students to develop a facility with words is to regularly expose them to words in a meaningful context. Think of a spelling bee; participants often ask for the word to be used in a sentence. The sentence provides a context, a necessary link between the word and the students' prior knowledge and experiences. The more a student uses a word in different contexts, the more likely the student will be able to add it to his or her personal lexicon of words.

Activities in this chapter have been carefully developed to give students a fresh approach to vocabulary learning. Students who have experienced difficulty reading need novel ways to study words. You are encouraged to select activities that meet the unique interests and needs of your students. Whenever possible, look for ways to connect vocabulary to your students' prior experiences.

Guidelines for instruction and activities for learning are divided into two sections: direct instruction and contextual instruction. Whether you begin with direct instruction or contextual instruction will depend on the needs of the students in your class.

DIRECT INSTRUCTION GUIDELINES

Through direct instruction, teachers systematically impart information to their students. Basic skills are often taught in isolation so students can become proficient with each piece of the learning before it is placed into a context. This enables students to focus directly on the material they are trying to learn without being distracted or overwhelmed by too much information at one time.

Guiding Principles for Direct Instruction

1. When teaching new words, provide concrete materials or visuals to enhance meaning; connect words to the students' lives.

2. Encourage verbal and written wordplay by creating a print-rich classroom environment.

3. Show students how to find words in the dictionary. For students who use the dictionary frequently, provide a personal copy to simplify this task. Make sure students know how to use the dictionary efficiently.

4. Encourage students to talk about ways they learn new words. Let them discuss the words and the strategies they use with the whole class, a partner, or another student having trouble learning words. Not only do students crave socialization with their peers, but peers make excellent teachers.

5. Provide multiple opportunities for students to review targeted words and their definitions.

Direct Instruction Activities (language arts standards 3 and 6)

1. Create a word ceiling. After introducing words from the film, write them on separate pieces of paper using a medium-point marker so words are easily read from a distance. Tape the words to the ceiling. You may add simple definitions next to the words. Leanne, a remedial reading teacher at Senatobia Junior High School in Senatobia, Mississippi, began posting words on the ceiling when she saw how many of her students sat back in their chairs and stared at the ceiling!

2. Provide students with a list of vocabulary words from the film. Direct them to arrange words by length, first letter, or parts of speech (nouns, verbs, adjectives, and adverbs). Use these ideas to create other categories for word manipulation. (Adapted from Robb, Klemp, & Schwartz, 2002)

3. Give one to three vocabulary cards to the students before the film. As students view the film, direct them to look for words in the subtitles that are the same as the words on their cards. As students match the words from the film with the words on their cards, they are to turn the cards face down on their desks. The goal is to have no cards face up at the end of the viewing. Have students choose one word card and describe how the word was used in the film.

4. Yes/No/Why (Beck, Perfetti, & McKeown, 1982): Pair vocabulary words from the film according to names of characters, places, categories of items such as food or weapons, parts of speech, number of syllables, synonyms, first letter, and so forth. Show the students a set of two words from the vocabulary list. Ask students to determine whether the two words can be paired together. For each set of words, students say "Yes" if the words can be paired and "No" if the words cannot be paired. For each yes or no answer, students must explain why. *Hint: If students initially need guidance, state the category you selected for the set of words. After students gain experience with this activity, direct them to pair words according to criteria they develop.

5. When introducing the film, give a brief overview of the plot based on the outline of events in the film guide. Look for ways to relate aspects of the plot to prior course content and events in the students' lives. Ask students to predict which words they are likely to encounter during the film using clues from the title and overview of the film. Make a list of words based on the students' predictions and post them in a prominent location. After viewing the film, ask students to tell you the words they remember seeing. Write these words and compare them with their list of predicted words. Keep all words related to the film in a prominent place for students to read.

6. Have students participate in a modified spelling bee. Name a word and have the student use the word in a sentence. Or, read a definition, and ask students to name the word.

7. Play Vocabulary Bingo with vocabulary definitions and sentences. You may add other words tailored to your class as students watch the film. (Adapted from an idea by Allison Movitz, Bruce High School, Bruce, Mississippi)

8. Let your students play Scrabble. Give students generous bonus points every time they form a word from the subtitles of the film they are watching.

9. Create cards based on the game of Memory. Select up to 12 words from the vocabulary film list. Make a deck of 24 cards. Write a word or phrase on 12 cards and their definitions on the other 12 cards. Randomly spread all of the cards face down on a table. A student picks a card, reads it, and tries to pick the matching card. If he does not find a matched set, he must return the cards face down on the table, and the next student begins to play. Students continue playing until they do not pick a matched set. At the end of the game the person with the most matched sets wins. Pictures or illustrations may be substituted for the written word cards. (Cheryl Grisham, Senatobia Junior High School, Senatobia, Mississippi)

10. Make a game based on the popular TV show *Password*. Students work in pairs. One student reads a word from the film to herself and gives a clue about the word to the other student (e.g., for the word *colony* a clue could be "established by the English"). If the student guesses the word

colony in one try, she earns five points. Lower the points earned for each successive guess. (Cheryl Grisham, Senatobia Junior High School, Senatobia, Mississippi)

11. Story Puzzles (adapted from Miller, 2001): Choose a puzzle with 25 pieces. (Teachers should mark the back of one of the pieces as a free piece.) Write words and their corresponding definitions on adjacent puzzle pieces. To work the puzzle, students put together the words and definitions.

12. Create a classroom word wall. Encourage students to watch for words in the movie that they would like to add to the word wall. Create lists of words that fit a particular category (e.g., forms of government, names of countries or locations, food, types of money, and types of weapons). Label each category and place words under the correct category. A simple form of a word wall is a large whiteboard with markers. By using a whiteboard, you and your students have the flexibility of easily adding and rearranging words.

13. Give students a list of vocabulary words from the movie. Ask students to write a word that they know is similar to the new word and explain their word choice.

14. Choose six words from the film's vocabulary list. Have students interact with these words before, during, and after the film.

a. Before the film, display a sign that says "Now Showing." Post approximately five or six new vocabulary words on this sign. Review the words with the students, and direct them to watch for the words as they view the film.
b. During the film, encourage students to share words they have seen that match the words on the "Now Showing" sign. Please note, this is a good opportunity to point out targeted words as they appear, but be careful not to disrupt the flow of the story.
c. After the film, have students relate words they saw in the subtitles to the words on the "Now Showing" sign. Have students suggest other words they read in the subtitles that they would like to add to the sign.

15. Have a contest! Each day in small groups direct students to list as many words (four letters or more) as they can recall from the subtitles in

two minutes. Provide time for students to share and discuss words and definitions in their groups. Collect students' lists, and at the end of the week tally the total number of words each group wrote. Type the words on a bookmark for the group who listed the most words. If possible, laminate bookmarks and give to each member of the class.

16. Have students select five words from the subtitles. Write the words across the board. Make a bar graph that illustrates the levels of difficulty indicated by the students. Have students vote on the word they think is most difficult to read and understand, and graph their responses (see figure 3.1). Some students will see they are not alone in thinking some words are difficult; others will experience success when they know a word others think is difficult. Difficulty may be based on pronunciation, spelling, or meaning. (Adapted from Robb, Klemp, & Schwartz, 2002)

17. Construct and deconstruct words. List words with prefixes and suffixes from the film's vocabulary list on the board. Ask each group to choose three words. Their task is to make new words by adding or subtracting different prefixes and suffixes for each word.

18. Categorization: Choose a category (e.g., synonyms, antonyms, alliteration, assonance, consonance) and write a list of three words that fit the category and one word that does not fit the category. Students find the unrelated word and explain why it doesn't fit.

19. Ask students to write a correct definition for a word from the film and a bogus definition. Collect their definitions and read them to the class. The class decides which definitions are correct and which definitions are

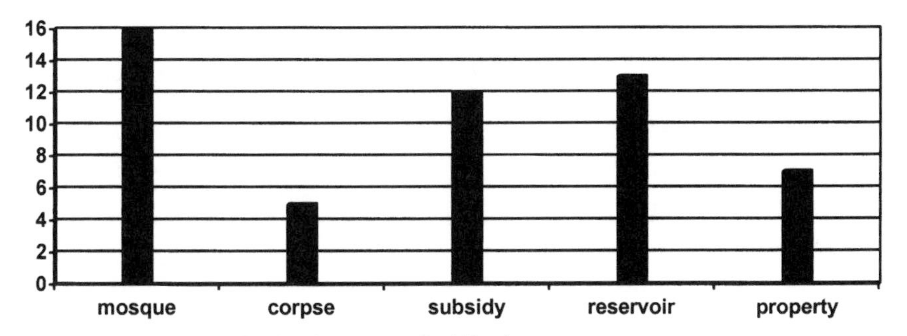

Figure 3.1. Bar Graph of Relative Word Difficulty

bogus. "This activity has had some hilarious results," according to Allison Movitz at Bruce High School.

20. Make or purchase Whisper Phones. Students read and practice words and definitions without disturbing others by whispering into their phones. Whisper Phones are made from two pieces of PVC pipe connected to look like a telephone receiver. They are inexpensive to buy, about $2.50 per phone, and even cheaper to make, under $1.00 per phone. Whisper Phones can be purchased from school supply catalogs or the Internet. PVC pipe is easily found in home supply sections of stores. Though typically used in the lower grades, high school teachers have found them very useful for reading and vocabulary practice with older students.

CONTEXTUAL VOCABULARY GUIDELINES

Students gain a deeper understanding of a word's meaning if they can connect it to elements surrounding the text. Context clues in the form of prior events, surrounding text, and pictures help the reader create meaning from the text.

Guiding Principles for Contextual Learning

1. Use opportunities for students to see, hear, and use new words in a familiar context.

2. Provide opportunities for students to use new vocabulary during class.

3. Use writing to learn and reinforce reading vocabulary.

4. Provide a variety of contexts for students to interact with vocabulary.

5. Let students know it is okay to skip some words as they read. Struggling readers spend time trying to read every word in a passage. This causes students to lose sight of the meaning behind the rest of the words in the passage. Model reading while skipping some words. If the students see you selectively skip words as you read, you implicitly have given them permission to skip over words.

6. Provide opportunities for students to explore and learn words together.

Contextual Vocabulary Activities (language arts standards 3, 6, and 11)

1. Cut up words from phrases or sentences taken from the movie's subtitles. Put them in envelopes and have students reassemble the phrase or sentence. The same can be done with paragraphs from the movie. Cut the paragraph into sentence strips and ask students to arrange the sentences in a meaningful order. *Hint: Color code the words and strips that go with each phrase, sentence, or paragraph to avoid a colossal mixed-up mess of words and sentences.

2. Draw-a-Word: Choose words that lend themselves to visualization. Post these words (about five) in front of the class. Students work in pairs to draw pictures that represent the words. You can add some fun by having the students who finish all their words first yell "Diggle snort" or some other word or phrase that would be fun for the students. After they yell "Diggle snort," the students must read their words and explain the drawings to win. Like Bingo, if students are unable to read and explain all their words, the game continues until the next group yells "Diggle snort." Prizes can be awarded to the winning team.

3. Have students keep a journal. In one section they write a brief summary of the story they saw that day; in another section they write a prediction about what they think will happen next. Give recognition to students who include at least three words from the film in their writing. Have students highlight or otherwise mark these words in their journals.

4. Write sentences from the film's subtitles that contain the vocabulary you wish to teach. Give the sentences to each student. Write the vocabulary words contained in the sentences on a list for students to read. Direct students to read the sentences, find, and highlight the vocabulary words.

5. Write several passages as they appear in the subtitles. Choose a word from one of the passages and show it to the students. Direct students to use context clues from the film to arrive at a definition.

6. Choose a scene from the film and let students write a brief script. Give each group one or more words from the film. They are to use the word or words at least three times in their script. Provide time for students to practice reading the script and presenting their scene to the class. If possible use a video camera to record students as they act out their scripts. Show the film to the class.

7. Charades: Write words suitable for dramatization. Have one student act out a word from the film while the rest of the students guess the word. For additional reading practice, one student can record the words guessed by the class on the board or a large sheet of paper.

8. Have students identify with a character by choosing a character and an action he or she took. Students write about what they would have done if they had been in the same situation.

9. Design a poster advertising the film you have seen. Use as many vocabulary words in a meaningful way as you can. Recognize the individual or group that uses the most words in a meaningful way.

10. Write several vocabulary words or phrases from the subtitles on cards. Direct a student to choose a card and read it to the class. Students are to describe the context in which the word was used in the film. As a variation, students can identify the character that said the word or phrase.

11. Carousel Brainstorming (Rick Wormeli, 2001, p. 197): Place posters with keywords or topics from the film's subtitles around the room. Have students rotate among the posters, recording their thoughts and responses to whatever is written on the posters.

12. Show an illustration related to a concept from the movie. For example show a picture of a concentration camp for the movie *Life Is Beautiful*. Ask students to write or state all the words they can think of that go with the picture. Record the words next to the picture, and display it for extra reading practice and review.

13. After each showing of a part of the film, write a sequence of events on sentence strips. Post the sequence of events in the classroom to be used as a review and for discussion. Add to the sequence each time students view a portion of the film.

14. Students become film critics in the tradition of Siskel and Ebert by giving the film a "thumbs up" or "thumbs down" rating. Provide a paper divided down the middle. Label one side "Two Thumbs Up" and the other side "Two Thumbs Down." Ask students to rate the film and write a brief statement justifying their rating. Encourage students to use words from the film in their written statements.

15. Display words from the film on a word wall or conspicuous place. Direct students to create a reading map using words from the subtitles. Beginning with an oval or other shape in the middle, write the name of the film or a character. Connect smaller ovals to the center shape. Label each oval with something to do with the story. (See figure 3.2.) Here are some sample activities:

a. Students describe the parts of a story, characters, setting, problem, and resolution.
b. Students write events in chronological order, moving clockwise around the center shape.
c. Students choose and write a character from the film in the center shape. Students write descriptive words about each character in ovals surrounding the character's name, or they can recreate scenes from the film from the perspective of the character.

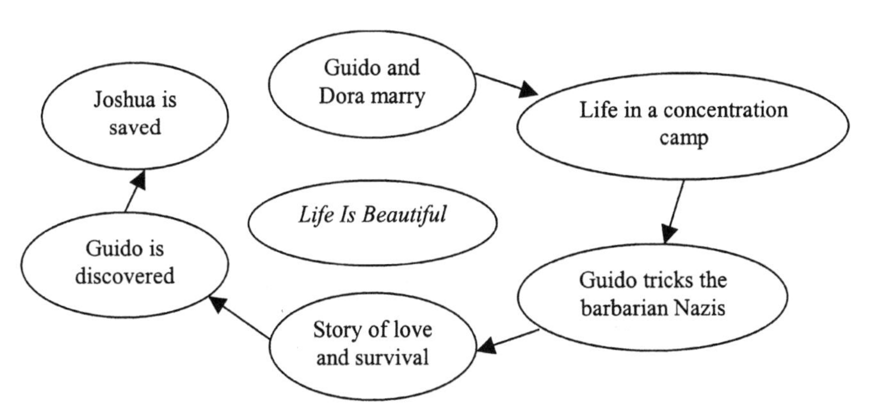

Figure 3.2. Sequence and Subject Organizer

16. Ask students to make predictions about the story and compare their predictions with the events as they unfold. Provide time for students to revise their predictions based on the new information from the film. Discuss students' predictions by asking the following questions:

What clues did you use to make your prediction?
What surprised you about the events in the film?
What do you think will happen next?

17. Have students examine cause and effect by choosing an action of a character (cause) and determining the effect of the action. For a variation, have students change an action and determine the logical effect of the new action.

18. To release students from the responsibility of reading and understanding every word, give students a copy of the following verses.

The Owl and the Pussy-Cat (last verse)
Dear Pig, are you willing to sell for one shilling
Your ring?
Said the Piggy, "I will."
So they took it away and were married next day
By the Turkey who lives on the hill.
They dined on mince, and slices of quince,
Which they ate with a runcible spoon;
And hand and hand, on the edge of the sand,
They danced by the light of the moon,
The moon,
The moon,
They danced by the light of the moon.

—Edward Lear

The Jabberwocky (third verse)
He took his vorpal sword in hand:
Long time the manxome foe he sought
So he rested he by the Tumtum tree,
And stood awhile in thought.

—Lewis Carroll

The words *mince*, *quince*, and *runcible* from the first poem and *vorpal*, *manxome*, and *Tumtum* from the second poem are not common words; some are nonsense words made up by Edward Lear and Lewis Carroll. However, students can make sense of these poems without understanding all of the words. The fun and meaning of the poems are possible because of context clues provided by the surrounding words.

VOCABULARY WEBSITES

1. Vocabulary strategies:
University of North Carolina at Wilmington, *Vocabulary Strategies*, people.uncw.edu/sherrilld/edn356/notes/vocabulary_strategies.htm
All America Reads, www.allamericareads.org/lessonplan/vocab.htm

2. Motivating low-performing adolescent readers:
All America Reads, *Motivating Low-Performing Adolescent Readers*, www.ericfacility.net/ericdigests/ed396265.html

3. Teaching vocabulary to adolescents to improve comprehension:
Teaching Vocabulary to Adolescents to Improve Comprehension, www.readingonline.org/articles/curtis

REFERENCES

Allen, J. (1999). *Words, words, words: Teaching vocabulary in grades 4–12.* Portland, ME: Stenhouse.

Beck, I. L., Perfetti, C. A., & McKeown, M. G. (1982). Effects of long-term vocabulary instruction on lexical access and reading comprehension. *Journal of Educational Psychology, 74*, 506–521.

Holmes, K. (2003). Show, don't tell: The importance of explicit prewriting instruction. *The Clearing House, 76*, 241.

Miller, W. (2001). *The reading teacher's survival kit.* West Nyack, NY: Center for Applied Research in Education.

Robb, L., Klemp, R., & Schwartz, W. (2002). *Reader's handbook: A student guide for reading and learning.* Wilmington, MA: Houghton Mifflin.

Wormeli, R. (2001). *Meet me in the middle: Becoming an accomplished middle school teacher.* Portland, ME: Stenhouse.

Chapter Four

Language Arts and Social Studies Activities

Most activities in this chapter easily integrate reading, language arts, and social studies. For activities specific to a particular film, look in the individual film guides. The activities outlined in this chapter may be used with any film.

STORY GRAMMAR: CHARACTERIZATION

1. Describe the relationship between the protagonist and the antagonist. What is the central conflict? What are the goals of each person? What are their strengths and weaknesses? Describe advantages one has over the other. (language arts standards 2 and 3)

2. E. M. Forster (Hunt, 1988, p. 2067) labels characters as "flat" or "round" depending on how much of the character's personality is revealed to the reader by the author. "Flat" characters are one dimensional, with one dominant identifying trait. "Round" characters are multidimensional, with many identifying traits. Flat characters can add an interesting dimension to the story. They can be a caricature of a real person, often adding humor, or used in juxtaposition to the round character to provide opportunities for the round character to be portrayed as a complex individual. Round characters usually reflect personality traits true to human nature. Characters may change during the course of the story. To label them "flat" or "round" requires consideration of the story as a whole. The following activities are best completed after the film has been seen in its entirety:

a. Identify characters as being either "flat" or "round." List the dominant trait of the flat character. What purpose does he or she have in the story? Does the flat character add to or detract from the story?
b. List dominant traits of the round character. Rewrite part of the story by exchanging "flat" and "round" portrayals of the characters. (language arts standards 3 and 6)

3. If the film is based on real events, choose a historical figure to research using the library and the Internet. One half of the class writes a list of questions for an interview to give to the other half of the class to an-

swer. Answers can be given orally or in writing. (language arts standards 4, 5, 7, and 8; social studies standards II and IV)

4. Choose an issue and write a speech for one of the main characters in the film. Practice the speech, working to get the character's point of view across to the audience. Practice using a dramatic oratory style. Watch speeches given today to learn techniques used by others to sway an audience. (language arts standards 4, 7, and 8; social studies standards II, IV, and IX)

STORY GRAMMAR: SETTING, TIME, AND PLACE

1. Use a map to locate the country that is the setting for the film. Determine its shape. Use a metaphor or simile to describe and compare the shape of the country. For example, France is like a starfish. Encourage students to use their imaginations to come up with approximations of a shape rather than perfect likenesses. (language arts standards 2 and 8; social studies standard III)

2. Locate major bodies of water, if any, that are adjacent to the country's borders and that are within the country. Include oceans, lakes, and rivers. Describe the topography of the country. (language arts standard 8; social studies standard III)

3. Determine the population density of the area depicted in film. Considering the topography, analyze the reasons for the country's population distribution. (language arts standards 7 and 8; social studies standard III)

4. Research the climate of the geographical area that is the setting for the film. State the impact of the climate on agricultural products, manufacturing, mode of dress, recreational activities, housing, and transportation. (language arts standards 7 and 8; social studies standard III)

5. Compare the area and population density of the country from the film with a particular state. (social studies standard III)

6. Describe how the director used the setting to convey information when introducing the characters and the problem the characters face. If a

prologue is shown at the beginning, tell what relevant information was given that described the setting, the characters, and the problem of the story. (language arts standard 2; social studies standard III)

7. While viewing the film, pause the film during a visually descriptive scene.

a. Analyze the scene to determine whether it conveys information concerning the era, location, cultural aspects, and mood.
b. Illustrate the scene, adding features you think would add meaning to the film.
c. Write a description of the scene using descriptive words to "paint a picture" for the reader. (language arts standard 6; social studies standards III and IV)

STORY GRAMMAR: PLOT AND SEQUENCE

A plot conveys a story by connecting one event to another, a "chain of causes and effects" (Hunt, 1988, p. 2082).

1. Write a list of the main plot and subplots. Label the plots as main or subplots. Determine whether they intertwined or changed in dominance during the story. (language arts standard 3)

2. Describe the way the main plot is introduced. (language arts standard 6)

3. Identify the essential problem. List events about the problem that occurred during the rising action. (language arts standard 6)

4. Identify the climax of the plot. (language arts standard 6)

5. List events that occurred during the falling action. (language arts standard 6)

6. Describe the dénouement (solution) of the plot. (language arts standard 6)

7. Gustav Freytag (Hunt, 1988, p. 2083) introduced a pyramid as a means to map the stages of a plot. Beginning at the base and ascending to the point of the pyramid are the introduction of the plot and rising action. The climax,

or resolution of the problem, occurs at the top of the pyramid. After the climax, falling action is depicted descending on the opposite side of the pyramid, followed by the dénouement, or solution. Because plots vary in the length of the introduction, rising action, climax, falling action, and dénouement, shapes representing a particular plot will vary. A roller coaster, with its quiet beginning, ascent to the top, the climax of seeing the twists and turns below, and the descent followed by the aftermath as the roller coaster rolls to a stop, may provide a more visually exciting way for students to represent the stages of the film's plot. Encourage students to think of a metaphor or simile to explain the plot of the film. Using the pyramid, roller coaster, or an original metaphor or simile, draw an appropriate graphic that reflects the stages of the plot of the film. (language arts standards 1, 2, 3, and 6)

8. After studying the graphic representation of the plot of the film, determine whether the plot could have been made stronger by lengthening or shortening any of the stages of the plot. (language arts standard 6)

9. Write a sequence of events on individual sentence strips. Post the sequence of events in the classroom to use as a review and for discussion. Add to the sequence of events each time students view a portion of the film. (language arts standard 6)

10. After each viewing of the film, write a significant event on a strip of paper. Sequence the events, illustrate them, and bind them into a book to share with other grades and classes. (language arts standards 5 and 6)

11. Choose a major character from a film that is based on real events. Identify the problem faced by the main character. Rewrite the action taken by the character. Describe the effects of the revised action. How would the course of events be altered? (language arts standards 6 and 7; social studies standards II and IX)

IMAGERY: CONVEYING MEANING THROUGH A SENSORY EXPERIENCE

1. Imagery involves the senses of hearing, seeing, tasting, smelling, and touching, as well as kinesthetic experiences. Determine ways the director used imagery to convey meaning. (language arts standards 3 and 6)

2. Contrasts are an important way to create imagery. Consider the following lines from *Twelve Paper Cows*, a Russian spy novel by John Holmes (2004, p. 111).

> "The pair strolled past an old dilapidated apartment building with peeling walls and broken window glass. It was surrounded by scaffolding and a dirty wooden fence. Across the street, standing in stark contrast, was a four-star hotel with majestic neo-Tsarist columns and clean walls. The dilapidated building was dark as a black hole; the four-star hotel glimmered with the radiance of many hidden lamps placed on and around its structure."

Identify a scene from the film that illustrates contrast. Describe how the contrasted scene provides a more powerful understanding of the setting and events. (language arts standards 2, 3, 5, and 6)

3. Choose a scene from the film. Rewrite the scene, using imagery to convey meaning. Use descriptive words that express sensory information. (language arts standards 2 and 6; social studies standard IV)

Examples: The crunch of the smooth red apple caused a sweet spray of sticky fragrant juice. The soil was tilled to a fine soft powder, smelling like life itself.

DIRECTOR'S GOALS

1. Write one sentence describing the dominant theme of the film: *The story is about one person's hard work and ambition being thwarted by another person's greed.*

Rewrite the description using half as many words: *The story is about ambition and greed.* Choose one or two words from the description that convey the theme: *ambition* and *greed*. (language arts standards 3 and 6)

2. From the theme, determine a universal truth that it conveys: *Greed can destroy the ambition of a person.*

Relate the universal truth to current events. (language arts standards 6 and 7)

3. Determine the tone or tones the director conveyed in the film through the spirit of the words, music, and background. Some tones the director

may want to convey include serious, lighthearted, resigned, hopeless, loving, evil, informational, or suspenseful. Determine the director's attitude toward the subject based on the tone of the film. (language arts standard 6)

4. Choose an event in the film. Rewrite the event using a different tone to convey meaning. (language arts standards 5 and 6)

5. After watching the film and considering the message the director was conveying, determine whether the name of the film supported the director's goals. Write three alternative titles to convey the director's message. Display the titles and determine the best titles for the film. (language arts standard 6)

POINT OF VIEW

1. Rewrite or tell the story from the different points of view of the characters in the film. To get into the spirit of the assignment, pretend to actually be the character. From the character's point of view, tell the story in a diary or a letter. (language arts standards 4, 5, and 6; social studies standard IV)

2. Choose an inanimate object from the film (e.g., train, plow, sword). Direct students to write a passage about the film from the object's point of view. (Allison Movitz, Bruce High School) (language arts standards 4, 5, and 6)

3. Often the reader knows more about events in the story than any single character. The point of view of the reader is often omniscient, privy to the thoughts as well as the actions of the characters. Dramatic irony is when the readers know something the characters do not. Because the reader is all-knowing, the reader can change the course of events. Choose a character and an event in his or her life. From an omniscient point of view, make recommendations to the character and describe how the recommendations change the story. (language arts standards 3, 5, and 6; social studies standard IV)

4. The dramatic point of view is limited to the actions of the characters but not their thoughts. Therefore, the reader may question why the

characters act as they do. Choose a character whose actions are difficult to understand. Write accompanying thoughts to explain and support the actions taken by the character. For example, in *War and Peace*, Napoleon led his army thousands of miles away from France, thus risking their well-being and ultimate survival. Describe possible thoughts that would lead Napoleon to take such drastic measures. (language arts standards 3 and 6; social studies standard IV)

CAUSE AND EFFECT

Examine cause and effect. Use a paper divided down the middle. At the top of the paper write the name of a character from the film. Label one section "Cause" and the other section "Effect." Choose an action or circumstance of a character (cause) and determine the effect of the action or circumstance (see table 4.1). For a variation, change an action and determine the logical effect of the new action. (language arts standards 6 and 7; social studies standard II)

MAKING INFERENCES: READING BETWEEN THE LINES

1. Look for examples of dialogue or events that do not explicitly provide detailed information, then infer meaning from the statements or events. Inferences can be organized on a simple chart. Table 4.2 provides examples based on the film *Life Is Beautiful*. (language arts standards 1, 2, 3, and 7)

Table 4.1. Cause and Effect Chart

Name of Character: Guido	
Cause	*Effect*
Guido was Jewish and lived in Italy during WWII.	Guido and his son were sent to a concentration camp.
Guido's wife, Dora, was not Jewish.	Dora had to beg to go to the concentration camp.

2. Passages from books or songs that appeared in the subtitles have been included word for word in the film guide. To promote success and fluency, it is advisable for students to read and review these passages before they occur in the film. Have students infer meaning from the passages before, during, or after viewing the film. (language arts standards 1, 2, and 3)

MAKING PREDICTIONS

1. Before beginning the film, discuss the title and describe the setting. Provide a brief background of the film. Predict the major problem in the story. Post students' predictions and review them periodically to determine how close their predictions were to actual events in the film. This can be done each day before showing the film. (language arts standards 3 and 6)

2. After viewing a segment of the film, write a prediction about what will happen next. Stop the film at the climax of the action. Write a prediction about the ending of the film. (language arts standards 3 and 6)

3. After watching the film, compare the students' predictions with actual events. Ask students to support their predictions by asking the following questions:

What clues did you use to make your predictions?
What surprised you about the events in the film?
How close were your predictions to the actual events in the film? (language arts standards 3 and 6)

Table 4.2. Event and Inference Chart

Event	*Inference*
Guido's bookstore did not have many customers.	(Students infer possible explanations.)
There were no children in the concentration camp.	
"No Jews or Dogs."	

FORESHADOWING

1. Identify aspects of the film that foreshadow future events. (language arts standards 3 and 6)

2. Based on the foreshadowing, predict future events. Write an outline of predictions and compare them with the events in the film. (language arts standards 3 and 6)

CRITIQUING THE FILM

1. Write a critique of the film. Include information about the characters, dialogue (including the author's choice of words), setting, and plot. (language arts standards 1 and 6)

2. Determine the purpose of the film. Did the director establish a clear sense of purpose? What elements of cinematography did the director use to support the purpose? (language arts standard 6)

3. After analyzing the story grammar of a plot, use Freytag's pyramid (see page 34) to determine whether the director developed each stage of the plot adequately. Which part of the plot could have been changed to make the film more comprehensible or interesting? Rewrite, adding or subtracting pieces of the plot to make the story stronger. (language arts standard 6)

SHARING THE STORY

1. List one event from the film that is meaningful. Share this event with a partner and discuss. (language arts standard 11)

2. Working in small groups, write a script about a brief scene from the film. Present the scene using props and music. (language arts standards 4, 5, and 6)

3. Share feelings the film evoked. Determine how the director used words, music, scenery, events, and lighting to create the mood of the story. (language arts standard 6)

4. Working in small groups, dramatize a scene from the film. (language arts standards 4 and 6)

5. After viewing the film, create a class outline of the film. Write a backward summary of the film, beginning with events from the dénouement and ending with the introduction of the plot. (language arts standard 6)

6. Accounts of history and current events are frequently written with a bias. Choose a point of view about an event from the film. Write two accounts: one account should be fact based and free of bias; the other should reflect your opinion. Read accounts of history and current events in newspapers and magazines. Determine whether they are fact based and free of bias or whether they reflect a point of view. When is it appropriate to write fact-based accounts? When is it appropriate to write opinion? Should the accounts be labeled factual and opinion, or should the reader beware? (language arts standards 1, 2, 3, and 12; social studies standard II)

7. Write to a pen pal from the country shown in the film. Recommend to your pen pal American films that best depict the culture of the American people. Many pen pal organizations are listed on the Internet. For example, ePALS Classroom Exchange has requests for pen pals, a book club, and a link to HarperTeacher.com, a website for educators and librarians. Some pen pal organizations charge a nominal fee. (language arts standard 12; social studies standards I and IV)

8. If students in your class come from a culture that is the same or similar to one shown in the film, invite them to bring in artifacts and share their culture with the class. Ask them to describe similarities and differences between the film's version of their culture and their personal experiences. (language arts standards 11 and 12; social studies standards I and IV)

9. Invite parents who have experienced a culture or time similar to the one in the film to share their stories and experiences with the class. Write questions for the guests prior to their arrival. Determine how cultures are affected by geographical location, institutions, era, religion, economics, social class, technology, and history. (language arts standards 11 and 12; social studies standards I, II, III, IV, V, VI, VIII, and IX)

REFERENCES

Holmes, J. (2004). *Twelve paper cows.* Baltimore: Publish America.
Hunt, D. (1988). *The Riverside anthology of literature.* Boston: Houghton Mifflin.

WEBSITES

Epals.com Classroom Exchange, www.epals.com
HarperTeacher.com, *Educators and Librarians*, www.HarperTeacher.com

Chapter Five

Film Guides

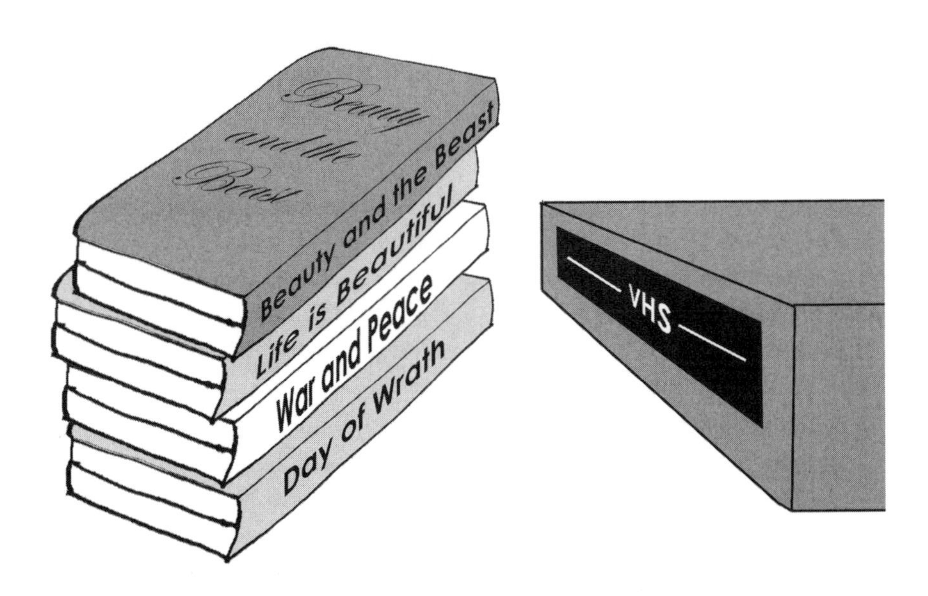

THE 400 BLOWS

Grade Level: 9–12
Time: 99 minutes
Filmed: 1959 in black and white
Language: French
Genre: Biographical drama
Director: François Truffaut
Rating: Not rated
Theme: One can overcome adversity in childhood with imagination and determination.
Interesting Fact: This story is loosely based on the early life of François Truffaut.
Setting: The streets, homes, schools, and detention centers in Paris, France, 1959.

Summary

Antoine Doinel is an adolescent trying to reconcile his life with the challenges of school, home, and peer pressure. Antoine's parents are constantly bickering, finding fault with each other and with him. His mother is cold and demanding; his father is ineffective at defending and soothing the effects of the constant criticisms and angry words that comprise Antoine's home life.

Life at school is no easier for Antoine. A harsh schoolmaster has apparently singled him out for humiliation and punishment. None of the authority figures in Antoine's life are supportive. To fit in with his friends, Antoine begins a life of petty crime and truancy. He tests the waters by stealing, skipping school, and running away from home. Even when Antoine's parents and school officials get angry, they do not seem to care about him. They are more concerned with the inconveniences to their lives and their images. While at the Observation Center for Juvenile Delinquents, Antoine reveals that his parents never wanted him. Emotionally, Antoine is truly alone. This movie is a coming-of-age film.

Characters

Antoine Doinel: A confused and rebellious 13-year-old boy seeking to become his own person.

Madame Doinel: Antoine's mother, married to M. Doinel. She is self-absorbed and sees Antoine as a nuisance.

Monsieur Doinel: Antoine's stepfather, who tries to be supportive but is ineffective.

René: Antoine's school friend who encourages truancy and helps Antoine when he runs away.

Teacher: Stern schoolmaster who shows his dislike for Antoine by revoking recess and punishing him in front of the class.

Outline of Events

1. The scene opens in a French school. Students are seen passing around a pinup picture while they are taking a test. Antoine gets caught and loses recess privileges. The schoolmaster, disliked by the boys, is taunted when his back is turned.

2. After school Antoine is expected to do chores for his mother. She is aloof and critical of his efforts. To compensate for the harsh treatment by his mother, Antoine's father tries to be friendly and lighthearted with him. Over dinner Antoine's parents try to decide what to do with him for the summer. They argue; Antoine overhears their discussion about sending him to boarding school.

3. The next day Antoine's friend René convinces him to skip classes. While playing around town they see Antoine's mother kissing another man. At home that night, Antoine's dad says that his mother will be working late; however, Antoine is not fooled. When his mother finally comes home after he has gone to bed, his parents fight again. His mother blames Antoine for all of her problems and threatens to send him away.

4. After Antoine misses school, one of his friends comes by his house to see if he is feeling better. Antoine's dad is angry, but his mother, knowing Antoine saw her with another man, tries to act unconcerned. The following day, Antoine fabricates a story, telling his teacher that he missed school because his mother died. He gets sympathy until both of his parents show up at school and expose his lie. After getting in trouble, Antoine decides he cannot live at home anymore. He writes his parents a letter and leaves to meet his friend René at his uncle's old printing factory, where he

plans to sleep. After reading Antoine's letter, his parents begin arguing, not about Antoine's absence but about whom Antoine likes better and what a nuisance he is.

5. Antoine is forced to leave the printing factory to avoid detection when workers arrive for their early morning shift. Once again Antoine is back out on the street. He steals some milk before going to school the next day. It is Christmastime, and the cheery lights and decorations amplify Antoine's loneliness. Without a home, Antoine is forced to steal food and drink water from fountains as he roams aimlessly from place to place.

6. Once again Antoine returns to school. While he is in class, his parents come for him. His mother, being overly solicitous, empathizes with Antoine's difficulties at school. She tells him, "Algebra, science, I know you learn useless things in school. Who needs it? But French . . . we all need to write letters." In her own way, she is trying to convince him of the merits of staying in school.

7. At home Antoine reads *The Quest of the Absolute* by Balzac and is inspired to write. He creates a small shrine and accidentally starts a fire with a candle he lit for Balzac. His father is angry, but his mom suggests they leave and go to a movie. The family experiences a brief moment of closeness. This episode of love and laughter stands in stark contrast to the usual hostile environment that surrounds Antoine. It is a poignant scene showing how good life could have been for Antoine and his family.

8. At school Antoine turns in a piece of writing that he copied from Balzac. The teacher gives Antoine an F on his paper for plagiarism. He is sent to the principal's office but runs away instead. Antoine's friend, René, talks back to the teacher and gets kicked out of class as well. Antoine and René run around the city, steal money from Antoine's grandmother, and go back to René's house. René says they will be safe there because his parents are rarely around. René sneaks food to Antoine. They continue to make mischief the next day and try to figure out how to make money.

9. Antoine and René decide to steal a typewriter from Antoine's father's office and pawn it. They are unsuccessful at pawning the typewriter, and Antoine gets caught trying to return it to his father's office. Antoine's fa-

ther is called and takes him to the police. Monsieur Doinel asks the police to do something with him because they no longer want to handle him. Antoine is put in jail.

10. Antoine's mother talks to the judge about bringing him home, but she admits they have no control. The judge challenges their parenting skills but offers little help. It is revealed that Monsieur Doinel is not Antoine's real father. Antoine's parents decide it is best for Antoine to be handled by the justice system. He is transferred to the Observation Center for Juvenile Delinquents.

11. At the center Antoine must talk to a psychologist. He reveals that he lived with his grandmother until he was eight, but when she got too old, he had to move back with his parents, even though they did not want him.

12. On visitation day, his friend René tries to come, but they won't let him in. His mother visits instead. She says she doesn't want him anymore and tells him they are sending him to labor camp. He runs away during a recess time and doesn't stop until he comes to the ocean, seeing it for the first time in his life. The desolate yet powerful ocean symbolizes the vast emptiness and freedom that is now Antoine's life.

Vocabulary

A lengthy list of words and phrases from the subtitles of this film is provided. From this list teachers can choose the words most appropriate for their classes. Words appear in chronological order so they may be introduced and reviewed as needed.

silence
take advantage
no exception
Michelin Guide
dismissal
incredible
mandatory
maximum punishment
unjustifiably punished
irresponsible
referee
insolent
conjugate
secret diary
recitation
concentrate
deface
arsonists

naturally
abominable
idiot
plagiarize
confesses
suspended
cowards
illegal
discrete
military academy
louse
uniform
surgery
kindness
scissors
persuasion
that's disgusting
punishment
promotion
vagrancy
inventory
Department of Juvenile Delinquents
bachelor
psychologist
aggressive
overheard
take initiative
criticized

Before the Movie

1. Antoine's class had to copy a poem from the blackboard. Write the following poem on the board to familiarize students with the words and meaning before they encounter it in the film.

The Hare
In the season when the thickets
Glow with flowers,
When the black tip of my long ears could be seen
Above the still green rye
From which I nibbled
The tender stems
As I played round.
One day that unaware
I was there fast asleep in my hutch
Little Margot surprised me.
She loves me so
My beautiful mistress.
She was tender and sweet.
How she hugged me on her lap and kissed me.
Better than thrones in the woods
Than flowers in the cradle.

Better to have freedom and feel a threat
Than slavery
With eternal April.
The dying man pulled himself up
And gave his children a piercing look.
His hair bristled on the nape of his neck;
His eyes lit up. A breath caressed his face and made it sublime.
He raised his hand with anger
And shouted Archimedes' famous last words
Eureka! I found it.

2. Discuss the meaning of the lines, "Better to have freedom and feel a threat than slavery with eternal April." How do you think the meaning of the poem relates to the theme of the film?

During the Movie

1. Why does Antoine seek freedom from home and school?

2. Who seems to have the most influence over Antoine's life?

After the Movie

1. In the movie there was a struggle between order and chaos. Give some examples of order and chaos.

2. What events led Antoine to try to leave his parents?

3. How did Antoine change from the beginning to the end?

4. What was the message of the movie?

Language Arts Activities

1. What do you think about the ending? Was it satisfying, or were you disappointed? Rewrite the ending in your own words; be creative. (language arts standard 5)

2. The movie focused on the French school system. Research the French school system and compare it with the American system. Consider

the positive and negative aspects of each. Write a proposal to your principal recommending changes to your school. Use your research as a basis for the proposal. (language arts standards 5 and 7)

3. Choose an event in Antoine's life. Imagine you are Antoine, and write a journal entry about your thoughts. (language arts standards 2 and 5)

4. Read a biography of François Truffaut's life. Compare his life with Antoine's life. Determine the similarities and differences. Based on Truffaut's biography, what facts would you choose to include in a story based on his life? (language arts standards 6, 7, and 8)

Social Studies Activities

1. Determine situations in the movie where there were civic and ethical decisions to be made. Discuss each situation, and make a chart showing the problems and solutions to the problems. (social studies standard X)

2. Think about the depiction of the French juvenile justice system. Research American and French juvenile justice systems. Create a plan for a juvenile justice system you think would be just, fair, and effective. (social studies standard VI)

3. Think about schools as an institution. Decide whether schools have a responsibility to help troubled children. Could the school have helped Antoine? What program does your school have for students with problems? Devise a program to help students like Antoine. (social studies standard V)

4. What cultural differences and similarities do you see between French children and American children? Make a Venn diagram. (social studies standard I)

Related Resources

Fiction

The Quest of the Absolute (La recherche de l'absolu) by Honoré de Balzac, translated by Ellen Marriage

Hole in My Life by Jack Gantos
As Ever, Gordy by Mary Downing Hahn
Where the Heart Is by Billie Letts
Bad Boy: A Memoir by Walter Dean Myers
Missing the Piano by Adam Rapp
Catcher in the Rye by J. D. Salinger
Maniac Magee by Jerry Spinelli
Rite of Passage by Richard Wright
Pigman and Me by Paul Zindel

AU REVOIR, LES ENFANTS

Grade Level: 9–12
Time: 104 minutes
Filmed: 1987 in color
Language: French
Genre: Biographical history
Director: Louis Malle
Rating: PG (moderately strong language; *Arabian Nights* passage has sexual overtones)
Theme: Even the slightest actions can have tremendous consequences.
Interesting Fact: This film is loosely based on the life of director Louis Malle, who reportedly was seen with tears streaming down his face during the debut of his film.
Setting: German-occupied France during 1944 in a Catholic boarding school outside of Paris.

Summary

The occupation of France by the Nazis brings the war even closer to a group of French school boys living in the countryside outside of France. The film opens with 12-year-old Julien tearfully saying good-bye to his mother as he is about to board a train that will take him to a Catholic boarding school after the winter break. Once at school Julien quickly falls back into the traditions and routines of the school. Father Jean, the head of the school, has enrolled three new boys. Unknown to their classmates, the boys are Jewish and are hiding from the Nazis. Julien becomes friends with one of the boys, Jean Bonnet.

The plot unfolds through the everyday lives of the boys living at school. Julien, unaware that his new friend is Jewish, slowly becomes aware of their religious differences and customs. Being only 12, Julien is unable to comprehend fully the tragedy and unease that consumes his new friend's life.

Julien and Bonnet become inseparable. After seeing the harassment of a Jewish man in a restaurant and finding a picture and letters from Bonnet's family, Julien begins to lose his childhood innocence while gaining insights into the dangers that drove Bonnet into hiding.

A vengeful act by a greedy kitchen worker, Joseph, sets events in motion for an unintentional betrayal by a young boy caught up in an adult world. For Julien, entering the adult world is swift and brutal as he deals with the irrevocable loss of his friend, Bonnet, because of a fateful glance.

After the war Julien (Louis Malle) learned that his friend, Jean Bonnet, and the other Jewish boys perished in Nazi concentration camps. Memories of that fateful day have remained with him throughout his life.

Characters

Julien Quentin: A 12-year-old Catholic boy who attends a Catholic boarding school with his brother. He becomes Jean Bonnet's best friend and ultimately and unwittingly betrays him.

Jean Bonnet (Jean Kippelstein): One of the three Jewish boys seeking refuge at a Catholic boarding school. He becomes Julien's best friend.

Father Jean: Head of the boarding school. He agrees to shield three Jewish boys from the Nazis.

Joseph: The cook's assistant. He uses his position to engage in black market activities and seeks revenge on Father Jean by informing the Germans about the Jewish people hidden at the school.

François: Older brother of Julien.

Madame Quentin: Mother of Julien and François. She is concerned about keeping her sons safe.

Negus and Dupré: Two other Jewish boys hiding from the Germans in the Catholic boarding school.

Outline of Events

1. Julien's mother drops him off at the train station after winter break so he can return to his Catholic boarding school. He wants to remain in Paris but is told that it is impossible. Whether Julien is sent to boarding school with his older brother because of the expectation of the bombing of Paris is left up to the viewer.

2. During the winter break, unknown to the other students, the head of the school, Father Jean, agrees to hide three Jewish boys at the school. Upon his return to the school, Julien meets one of the three new students, Jean Bonnet from Marseille.

3. At recess, while the boys play on stilts, a fight breaks out. Julien is injured and sent to Mrs. Perrin in the kitchen to tend to his wound. He makes arrangements with Joseph, a kitchen helper, to exchange his jar of homemade jam, given to him by his mother, for marbles. Unknowingly, Julien is participating in the black market.

4. A bomb drill sends the students to an underground bomb shelter where they begin to recite the "Hail Mary." Everyone, except Bonnet, recites the prayer. This, combined with other "strange" behaviors, including his refusal to eat pork pâté, arouses Julien's interest. He investigates Bonnet's personal belongings and finds a photo of Bonnet with his mother and father, as well as a book with the name Jean Kippelstein inscribed inside the cover. Julien realizes that Jean Bonnet is actually Jean Kippelstein, a boy of Jewish heritage.

5. Julien and Bonnet's friendship grows, and the two boys begin to spend more time together. Both Julien and Bonnet are at the top of their class. They are serious minded, enjoying books and music, which makes them targets of pranks and boyish insults.

6. During an outside scavenger hunt, Julien and Bonnet become lost in the woods and are eventually found by two German soldiers. Bonnet runs because he is certain they can tell he is Jewish. However, the German soldiers take both boys back to the school and remind Father Jean of the curfew rules. After their ordeal Julien and Bonnet are taken to the infirmary, where Julien confronts Bonnet about his true identity.

7. Julien invites Bonnet to go to lunch with his mother and brother. Only after they witness an incident between an elderly Jewish man and the Germans at a restaurant does Julien begin to understand the seriousness of Bonnet's secret identity.

8. Joseph is caught selling items on the black market and is fired. In his anger he tips the Germans to the possibility that Father Jean is using the Catholic boarding school to hide Jewish boys.

9. One fateful day while Bonnet and Julien are in class, the Nazis enter the classroom looking for the hidden Jews. Every movement inside the classroom stops. As the Nazis bellow questions and demands, Julien, in a moment of thoughtless action, steals a furtive backward glance at Bonnet. Instantly, Nazi soldiers approach Bonnet. Realizing he has been discovered, Bonnet quietly packs his books and supplies and is led away.

10. The Catholic boarding school closes. Everyone is told to pack his belongings. During the time Julien is packing, Bonnet arrives to gather his things under the bored yet menacing eye of a German soldier. Bonnet, trying to assuage his friend's guilt, says, "Don't worry, they would have gotten me anyway." Bonnet gives his collection of books to Julien. Julien removes the banned book *Arabian Nights* from under his mattress and gives it to Bonnet.

11. Julien returns to the infirmary and sees that Negus, another Jewish student, was hastily hidden under the covers of a bed. Two German soldiers enter the infirmary and ask whether any Jews are there. While Julien is being interrogated by one of the soldiers, the viewer is led to believe that the nurse, a Catholic nun, gives away the hiding place of Negus. Negus is caught and taken away.

12. Julien realizes that Joseph was the reason the Nazis raided the school. The Germans order everyone outside. As the boys are standing in front of the German soldiers, Father Jean and the three Jewish boys are seen leaving the school grounds. With a last wave, Bonnet says good-bye to his friend.

13. Off screen, Bonnet, Negus, and Dupré are taken to Auschwitz in Poland. Father Jean is taken to Mauthausen, a concentration camp in Austria. None survive.

Vocabulary

A lengthy list of words and phrases from the subtitles of this film is provided. From this list teachers can choose the words most appropriate for their classes. Words appear in chronological order so they may be introduced and reviewed as needed.

naughty
heretic
Mardi Gras
militia
all aboard
collaborates
vacation
shirkers
black market
exempt
whooping cough
good riddance
Memoirs of Sherlock Holmes
intelligent
fearless knight
competition
dangerous
hypocrite
continuous
Marseille
vitamin
expelled
lost my appetite
prisoners
quadrilateral
What happened?
tangents
civilian
air raid
Arabian Nights
cardboard muscles
You are disgusting
curfew
half-a-meat coupon
go to confession
ludicrous
vitamin deficiency
engineer
don't trust rumors
accountant
Gestapo
No Jews Allowed
betrayal
Protestant
Resistance leaflets

Before the Movie

1. Locate Paris, France, and Germany on a map. Trace the Nazi invasion of France.

2. How do you treat new students who arrive at your school?

3. How does it feel to be a new student?

During the Movie

1. Discuss the possible reasons that Julien and his brother François were sent to a Catholic boarding school.

2. Compare the differences between the French boarding school and your school.

After the Movie

1. The action of the film took place in 1944. How much longer would Bonnet and the other Jewish boys have had to remain hidden from the Germans before the end of the war?

2. Bonnet, Negus, Dupré, and Father Jean were sent to concentration camps in Poland and Austria. Determine the names of the camps and find their locations. How far did Bonnet, Negus, Dupré, and Father Jean have to travel to arrive at the camps?

3. Father Jean was a member of the French Resistance. Why would Father Jean and other men and women join the French Resistance? What were their goals?

Language Arts Activities

1. Julien was shown reading the following passage from a book while he was at the boarding school.

> Star of the sea
> Behold an ocean of wheat,
> And our granaries are piled high.
> Here you overlook the vast sheet,
> Your voice echoes over its length.
> Our absent friends left us desolate.
> Our hands hang out inanimate
> Idle and full of strength.

With no prior knowledge of what Julien was reading, interpret the text. What is meant by the passage? Describe the setting? Who do you think was speaking? Make up a story to accompany the passage. (language arts standards 2 and 3)

2. When Julien was looking in Bonnet's book, a letter dropped out and he read the following part:

> My darling,
> As you know it's hard for me to write to you.
> Mr. D was going to Lyon and he agreed to mail this.
> Your aunt and I seldom go out.

Read the letter and determine, based on the current political events, why it was hard for Bonnet's mother to write to him. Research ways the war affected people's lives and write an ending to the letter. (language arts standards 3, 5, and 7)

3. Bonnet mentioned that his father was a POW. Describe what you think happened to his father. Bonnet also mentioned he didn't know where his mother was. Discuss what you think happened to Bonnet's mother. (language arts standards 3, 4, and 7)

Social Studies Activities

1. Julien received the following letter from his mother:

> The apartment seems empty without you.
> Paris is not fun. They bomb us nearly every night.
> Yesterday a bomb killed eight people. Charming!
> The girls are back in school.
> Sophie works for the Red Cross.
> So many unfortunates.
> Dad's at the place in Lille.
> Business is bad and he's grouchy.
> It's time the war ended.
> I'll come visit you next week. We'll have lunch out.
> Hugs and Kisses
> Your loving mother,
> P.S. Eat your jam. I'll bring more. Take care.

Research life in Paris during 1944. Was Paris bombed during this time, and if so, was it the Allies or the Germans doing the bombing? Using information from the letter, describe what life was like for the citizens of Paris during the war. (social studies standards I and IV)

2. Julien learned that his father was working in Lille. There is a Lille, France, and a Lille, Belgium. Find both cities on a map. Read about both cities and determine where you think Julien's father was working. What were the primary industries and businesses in each city? What type of work do you think Julien's father was doing? (social studies standards III and V)

3. Bonnet's mother did not indicate where she was when she wrote a letter to her son. She did give one clue as to her whereabouts when she said, "Mr. D. was going to Lyon." Find Lyon, France on a map. How far is Lyon from Paris? Looking at a map, list the places where Bonnet's mother could have been when she wrote the letter. (social studies standard III)

4. Research the idea of black markets. What are black markets? Why would people risk buying and selling goods on a black market? What types of goods were sold on the black market during World War II? (social studies standard VI)

5. During World War II, many French people joined the French Resistance after Germany occupied more than three-fifths of their country in 1940. Research accounts of resistance fighters, and put together a timeline of their activities. Imagine you are a member of the resistance group. Identify your goals. Write an underground newsletter detailing the activities of your group. (social studies standards I, II, and V)

6. Different cultures have traditions that represent a rite of passage into adulthood. Identify some of the actions taken by Julien, his brother, and the other boys at the school that signified their desire to become adults. List some of today's traditions that are popularly used as rites of passage into adulthood. (social studies standards I and IV)

Related Resources

Fiction

Twenty and Ten by Clair Huchet Bishop
Jacob's Rescue: A Holocaust Story by Malka Drucker and Michael Halperin

The Good Liar: A Dramatic Story Set in Occupied France During World War II by Gregory Maguire
Friedrich by Hans Peter Richter
A Pocket Full of Seeds by Marilyn Sachs
Soldier X by Don L. Wulffson and Don Wulffson
The Devil's Arithmetic by Jane Yolen

Nonfiction

A Garden of Thorns: My Memoir of Surviving World War II in France by Roger de Anfrasio and Mark D. McKennon
Vive la France: The French Resistance During World War II by Robert Green
A Hero of Our Own: The Story of Varian Fry by Sheila Isenberg
The Fall of France: The Nazi Invasion of 1940 by Julian Jackson
No Pretty Pictures: A Child of War by Anita Lobel
Stones in Water by Donna Jo Napoli
The Lily Cupboard by Shulamith Levy Oppenheim
A Place to Hide: True Stories of the Holocaust Rescues by Jayne Pettit
Jews in France During World War II by Renée Poznanski and Nathan Bracher
The Courage to Care: Rescuers of Jews During the Holocaust by Carol Rittner
The Silent Hero: A True Escape Story From World War II by George Shea

BABETTE'S FEAST

Grade Level: 9–12
Filmed: 1987 in color
Genre: Drama
Rating: G
Time: 102 minutes
Language: Danish and French
Director: Gabriel Axel
Theme: The whole of a person is not apparent from the surface.
Interesting Fact: This movie is based on a story by Isak Dinesan, who also authored *Out of Africa* in 1985.
Setting: Frederikshavn, Denmark, 1834, a small community on the northeast coast of Jutland, the largest geographical region in Denmark. People exist on a simple diet of fish (herring and cod) and coarse dark ale bread.

Summary

Babette's Feast offers viewers a glimpse of life in a small coastal Danish town. Scenes of homes with thatched roofs, the tiny grocery store, mode of dress, transportation, and the preparation of food clearly illustrate 19th-century Danish life.

Philippa and Martina are daughters of a pious minister. Their calling, according to their father, is to lead a simple, pure life honoring God and serving the poor. The sisters, obeying the will of their father, give up opportunities for love and fame, remaining spinsters throughout their lives.

Babette, friend of one of Philippa's rejected suitors, lost her husband and son in the French civil war. She makes her way to the home of Philippa and Martina, willing to work and cook in exchange for room and board.

Years later, using money she won in the French lottery, Babette imports food from France to prepare a feast for the sisters and the members of the church. She imports live guinea hens, a sea turtle, wine, champagne, fresh fruit, and cheese from Paris to create a sumptuous feast unlike any experienced by the simple, pious people of the village. Babette works for days preparing the feast, while the Christians spend days praying they will not commit the sin of self-indulgence and gratification when faced with the temptations of food and drink. Throughout their lives, with a few slips here and there, these good people have willingly sacrificed worldly pleasures to honor God.

Philippa and Martina are concerned about using their father's house for worldly pleasures. They have a difficult time reconciling their puritan beliefs with the planned extravagance. Up until the time of the feast, they had sacrificed life's pleasures, doing their humanly best to lead simple lives of self-denial.

Characters

Philippa and Martina: Dutiful daughters who must make difficult choices between following their own dreams, honoring their father, and serving their God.

The father: Pastor of a strict religious group. He refers to his daughters as his right and left hands, causing them to forsake all chances for love and a life of their own.

Lieutenant/General Lorens Lowenhielm: Officer in the Danish Army who falls in love with Martina. He marries another, but never loses his feelings for Martina. He is an honorable man with a successful military career.

Achille Papin: French opera star with a heart and dreams as robust as his voice. After losing Philippa, he returns to France to live out his days in heartbroken solitude.

Babette Hersant: Refugee from France. She becomes the servant to Martina and Philippa.

Erik: Nephew of Babette.

Outline of Events

1. Two middle-aged sisters live alone tending to the poor. They are respected active members in a small Christian church in Denmark.

2. Through the special effect of morphing, the middle-aged sisters change before our eyes into beautiful young maidens. They are living a quiet puritan life with their father. Both sisters, being beautiful, attract the attention of the young men in the area, but in honor of their father, they rebuff the attention of the suitors.

3. Two suitors create lifelong heartbreak for the sisters. A young lieutenant in the Danish Army, Lorens Lowenhielm, and Martina fall in love. Martina, not wanting to leave her father, and Lorens, from a different world, part in a particularly poignant scene. Martina bears her suffering silently while the lieutenant angrily swears to move on with his life.

4. Philippa, singing in church, attracts the attention of a French opera star, Achille Papin. He not only proposes his undying love but also has dreams of making the talented Philippa into an international opera star. Achille spends hours helping Philippa develop her already beautiful voice and dreaming about a life of music and love.

5. Philippa, realizing she could never leave her father, writes a letter ending her relationship with Achille and has her father deliver it to him. In a devastating scene, Achille, who had been happily singing about his love for Philippa, abruptly stops singing upon receiving her letter. Heartbroken, he says, "Good-bye my life, good-bye my love." He returns to Paris, never to see Philippa again.

6. Returning to the present, the sisters are middle-aged women. Philippa and Martina live the same quiet life together as they did when their father was alive. They attend to the daily chores, help the poor, and are active in their church.

7. In 1871, Babette Hersant, fleeing from civil war in France, where she had lost her son and husband, is encouraged by her friend Achille to seek out Philippa and Martina in Denmark. She arrives unexpectedly on their doorstep during a heavy rainstorm—exhausted, penniless, and begging for work. The sisters take her in, though they themselves have no money to pay wages; all they can offer is room and board.

8. Babette, who speaks only French, quickly learns the Danish language and is shown by the sisters how to cook the two side dishes that make up the mainstay of their diet: boiled codfish and coarse dark ale bread. Babette's ability to save money by bargaining with the local merchants impresses the sisters.

9. After 14 years of living in Denmark, cooking and eating simple Danish fare, Babette learns that she won 10,000 francs in the French lottery. Longing for the exquisite delicacies from Paris, she asks the sisters for permission to prepare a French feast. Reluctantly the sisters agree to Babette's request, and immediately Babette orders a multitude of food and drink to be delivered from France. When the village people hear about the planned feast, there is a silent uproar; the food and drink represent the evil of indulgence.

10. The day the food arrives is a joyous occasion for Babette and an uneasy one for Philippa and Martina. After seeing the wine and overall splendor of the feast Babette is planning to prepare, Philippa has a nightmarish dream about the fires of Hell engulfing them as they indulge in worldly pleasures. She confides in her friends that she believes her father is looking down at the preparations for the feast and accusing them of using his house for a witches' Sabbath. The sisters are torn between their belief that gluttony and enjoyment are sinful and their agreement to let Babette fulfill her dream of preparing a French feast.

11. The day of the feast arrives and so does the now General Lowenhielm, former suitor of Martina. The general is accompanied by his aunt,

one of the invited guests. Babette cheerfully sets another place at the table for the extra guest. Because the general does not have such an acute sense of self-denial, he clearly enjoys every bit of the food and every drop of the wine. He voices his delight for the food but finds the other guests unresponsive, commenting only on the weather and farming. The townspeople, clearly struggling to ignore the repast in front of them, are betrayed by the obvious pleasure reflected on their faces and in their eyes.

12. After the feast, General Lowenhielm once again professes his undying love to Martina and then leaves by a donkey-drawn cart to return to his life. Both are sustained by their love for each other.

13. As the exquisite food and drink are consumed, the people in the village begin to feel closer to each other. They express thoughts, long repressed, confessing past transgressions. These righteous people, through a touch of a hand or a brief kiss, are now able to demonstrate mercy and love. Their feelings are eloquently articulated during the feast when Lowenhielm repeats a line from Philippa and Martina's father, "Righteousness and mercy kiss each other."

14. Babette confesses that she is poor again, having spent all her lottery money on the feast. She also reveals she was the head chef at the Café Anglais in Paris. This revelation forges a bond between Philippa, who gave up her art of singing, and Babette, who gave up her art of cooking. They realize they both had talents to "make the angels sing," yet the opportunities to share their talents with the world were dependent upon the men they loved, and these men were gone forever from their lives.

15. Philippa, Martina, and Babette return to their quiet unassuming life in a small rural town on the coast of Denmark.

Vocabulary

A lengthy list of words and phrases from the subtitles of this film is provided. From this list teachers can choose the words most appropriate for their classes. Words appear in chronological order so they may be introduced and reviewed as needed.

remote
unfortunate bearer
flush of youth
narrowly escaped
prophet
flee from Paris
founder
blood-stained hands
minister
cherished
disciples
deplored
interpret the Word
applauded and adored
French servant
beautiful soprano of the snows
puritan ladies
humble homage
extraordinary
significant
flowering fruit tree
let it soak
illusion
skilling (currency)
destinies
fourteen years
higher vision
rancid
creditors' letters
lottery ticket
parental lectures
wretched
pious aunt
schisms
insignificant
jealous
impossible
tormented
cut a brilliant figure
intolerance and disagreements
engraved in his memory
peace and brotherhood
vanished
congratulations
distinguished person
modest supper
Royal Opera in Stockholm
vanity
yearn
lemonade
magnificent
depraved
melancholy
storm abated
consent
fjord
forever devoted
culinary genius

Before the Movie

1. Discuss the ethics and lives of the Puritans who helped found our country.

2. How has religion affected your life? What sacrifices have you made for your family and for God? What sacrifices would you be willing to make?

3. Locate Jutland on a map. Predict the kinds of food people would most likely eat given its geographical location.

During the Movie

1. Why did the daughters abide by their father's wishes even when it meant giving up their own dreams? What are your duties to your parents?

2. How do you view the father? Why do you think he wanted to keep his daughters at home?

After the Movie

1. How did knowing Philippa and Martina as young women help you to know and understand them as middle-aged women?

2. What was the significance of the fiery dream Philippa had before the feast?

3. How does the statement "In this beautiful life, all things are possible" apply to your lives?

4. What is meant by the statement "An artist is never poor"? Think of the many ways you can be rich.

Language Arts Activities

1. Create a stick figure of yourself. Radiating around your figure, add the people and institutions to which you are responsible. For each person or institution, list major ways they have shaped your life's decisions. (language arts standard 3)

2. Using reference and recipe books as a guide, first plan a seven-course French dinner and then a comparable seven-course American dinner. Compare and contrast the two types of dinners. (language arts standard 1)

3. Read about Martin Luther and Philip Melanchthon, the namesakes of Martina and Philippa. Give a presentation about ways they embody the puritan beliefs seen in the movie. (language arts standards 1 and 2)

4. Explore issues and concepts deeply by asking and answering a string of if–then statements. Think of many plausible if–then scenarios. After exploring if–then scenarios, write an if–then story. (language arts standards 3, 5, and 12)

Here is an example:

> *If* Martina and Philippa honored their hearts over their father,
> *Then* they would have moved far away.
> *If* the daughters moved far away,
> *Then* the father would have been heartbroken.
> *If* the father were heartbroken,
> *Then* a lovely and compassionate woman would agree to marry him.

Social Studies Activities

1. Christianity played an important role in the movie. The religious fervor of Martina and Philippa required and enabled them to live a puritan life, with few creature comforts. Religious self-abnegation is not new, nor is it confined to 19th-century Denmark, or even to Christianity as a whole. Give modern-day examples of other forms of self-denial in the name of Christianity. Research medieval examples of self-denial. Research modern examples of forms of self-denial in the name of deities of other religions. Think of secular examples of self-denial in the modern world. (social studies standards I and V)

2. Continuity and change constitute one of the themes of the film. Using a Venn diagram, record the things that changed during Philippa and Martina's lives and the things that stayed the same. (social studies standard II)

3. Babette imported many supplies for her feast from France because they were not available in Jutland. Research landforms, weather, customs, religion, and economics to determine why Babette couldn't get her supplies in Jutland. (social studies standards I, III, and VII)

4. About 200 years before the film was made, the Thirty Years War took place in Denmark over religion. *Babette's Feast* provides a good background about the importance of the Protestant religion to the Danes. Research the Thirty Years War and look for other incidents that reaffirm the importance of religion. (social studies standards I, IV, and V)

Related Resources

Fiction

The Scarlet Letter by Nathaniel Hawthorne
The Crucible by Arthur Miller

Nonfiction

Parisian Home Cooking: Conversations, Recipes, and Tips From the Cooks and Food Merchants of Paris by Michael Roberts
Glorious French Food: A Fresh Approach to the French Classics by James Peterson

BEAUTY AND THE BEAST

Grade Level: 6–12
Time: 93 minutes
Filmed: 1946 in black and white
Language: French
Genre: Fantasy
Director: Jean Cocteau
Rating: Not rated
Theme: Beauty is only skin deep; the character of a man runs deeper.
Interesting Fact: *La Belle et la Bête* is based on French author Jeanne-Marie Leprince de Beaumont's story of a beautiful young girl and her love for a beast; the story first appeared in a children's magazine in 1757.
Setting: A simple manor in a small unidentified French town and the bizarre and pretentious castle of the Beast.

Summary

In this Cinderella-type story we are indeed expected to believe in the magic of roses and the love of a beast. A merchant, who is heavily in debt, has four grown children—three daughters and a son. One of his daughters, Beauty, is beautiful inside and out; the other daughters, Felicity and Adelaide, are shallow and greedy. The son, Ludovic, is a gambler, heavily in debt, and owes his father's furniture to the moneylender. Before knowing the extent of his financial problems, the father had promised each of his daughters a gift. Unlike her two selfish sisters, Beauty asks only for a rose.

Upon learning that all his money went toward paying his creditors, the father rides off in despair through a dense fog-shrouded forest and comes across the Beast's palace. While at the palace he sees a rose for Beauty and picks it. He is caught by the Beast and is told he must die or send one of his daughters in his place. The father promises to send one of his daughters and is allowed to leave.

Beauty comes to the Beast's castle, where a strange relationship develops. She is dazzled by the Beast's jewels and riches and begins to fall in love with his gentle nature. The Beast has the feelings of a man but exhibits many traits of an animal. Beauty is startled when she comes upon him lapping water from a pond and dismayed that he hunts and eats prey like an animal.

The Beast's love for Beauty will end in his death unless she is able to return his love. When Beauty demonstrates her love for him, the real man inside the Beast is revealed.

Although, this film is familiar and straightforward, its subtleties promote the obvious discussion of how one's true nature is more important than one's appearance. A careful viewing of the film unmasks the more subtle themes, such as irresponsibility as demonstrated by Ludovic's gambling; business relationships, illustrated by the merchant and his lender; as well as the role of prioritization as demonstrated by Beauty's utmost concern for her family.

Characters

Beauty: A fair-haired and tenderhearted woman who saves her father's life by taking his place at the home of the Beast.

The Beast, also Prince Ardent: A victim of his parent's disbelief in magic; only a loving look will help him return to be the handsome Prince Ardent.

Beauty's father: Stricken with bad health and financial misfortune, he sends his daughter to live with the Beast to save his own life.

Adelaide and Felicity: Malicious and vain older sisters of Beauty. They are ill mannered and short tempered.

Ludovic: Brother of Beauty who gambles away his family's assets. He detests his sisters Adelaide and Felicity and protects Beauty.

Avenant: Friend of Beauty's brother, Ludovic. He is smitten with Beauty and asks her to marry him.

Prince Ardent: Transformed by the death of the Beast. He resembles Avenant.

Outline of Events

Prologue:

> Children believe what we tell them, they have complete faith in us. They believe that a rose plucked from a garden can bring drama to a family. They believe that the hands of a human beast will smoke when he slays a victim, and that this beast will be ashamed when confronted by a young girl.
>
> They believe a thousand other simple things.
>
> I ask of you a little of this childlike simplicity and to bring us luck, let me speak four truly magic words, childhood's Open Sesame, "Once upon a time . . ."

1. Beauty chooses to stay home to do chores while her vain and petty sisters attend a concert. While they are away, Avenant, a suitor of Beauty's, asks for her hand in marriage. Beauty refuses, saying she must stay and care for her father, who has acquired enormous debt.

2. Good news: Beauty's father learns that one of his merchant's ships has come into port. The father, expecting profits from the cargo, believes he is rich. Before he leaves, he asks each of his daughters what she would like him to bring back for her. Both of Beauty's sisters ask for finery, while Beauty humbly requests only a rose.

3. Upon the father's arrival at the ship, he is informed that his profits have been distributed to his creditors. Dejected and penniless, the father begins his journey home. While riding through the forest in a thick fog he becomes lost and comes upon the Beast's castle. A door opens automatically, and he enters and finds himself surrounded by disembodied hands, roars from wild animals, and breathing statues with moving eyes. Undeterred, he sits down at a dinner table, eats the spread of delicacies in front of him, and falls asleep.

4. The father is awakened by animal noises and hastily leaves. He calls for his horse, and as he leaves, he sees a beautiful rose that he stops and picks to give to Beauty. From out of nowhere the Beast appears and tells

the father he must die for stealing the rose. As an exchange for the rose and his life, the father is told to send one of his daughters in three days.

5. Beauty, out of love for her father, reluctantly agrees to go to the Beast's palace to save his life. Frightened at her first meeting of the Beast, Beauty passes out. When she awakens, the Beast informs her of her only duty, to meet him for dinner every night promptly at 7:00. He also tells her that every night at 7:00 he will ask to marry her. Meanwhile, things are not going well at home. Beauty's father becomes ill, the furniture is removed from his home to pay for Ludovic's debt, and the two sisters complain bitterly about having to do farm work.

6. Beauty's life with the Beast becomes routine. Each night at 7:00 while dining, the Beast asks Beauty to marry him. However, his appearance and animal instincts make Beauty reluctant to accept his offer of marriage, though she is enchanted by the jewels the Beast brings to her.

7. As each day passes, Beauty grows fonder of the Beast but refrains from saying "yes" to his question of marriage. She is homesick and wants to see her father. She begs the Beast to allow her to return home. Before the Beast allows her to leave, he asks her whether she loves another man. Though angered by her honest reply about her love for Avenant, he allows her to leave.

8. Before Beauty leaves to go home, the Beast gives her the five secrets of his power: the rose, a mirror, the golden key, a horse, and a glove. The golden key opens the Pavilion of Diana, where the gold and jewels are stored. With these gifts, the Beast exacts a promise from Beauty that she will return in one week.

9. Beauty returns to her father's house and once again assumes her role of housemaid. She shows her sisters the jewels the Beast gave her, but when they touch them they turn to repulsive knotted cords. Her sisters, who are insanely jealous of Beauty, join Ludovic and Avenant in a plot to steal the Beast's treasures.

10. Adelaide and Felicity steal the golden key from Beauty while she is sleeping and give it to Ludovic and Avenant. They take the key and ride to the Beast's castle. Beauty, beginning to miss the amiable company of

the Beast, uses his magical glove to be transported back to his castle. Once at the castle, she realizes she forgot to bring the golden key. Once again, using the glove, she returns to her father's house for the key; it is nowhere to be found. Upset that she broke her promise to the Beast, she returns to find him and explain what happened. The Beast, thinking Beauty is not coming back, is heartbroken and dying of grief. Beauty finds him and cradles his head while comforting him.

11. When Avenant breaks into the Pavilion of Diana, where the Beast's treasure is stored, a statue of Diana comes to life and shoots and kills him with an arrow. At the moment of Avenant's death, the Beast is transformed into Prince Ardent, and Beauty and the Beast live happily ever after.

Vocabulary

A lengthy list of words and phrases from the subtitles of this film is provided. From this list teachers can choose the words most appropriate for their classes. Words appear in chronological order so they may be introduced and reviewed as needed.

arrow
devoured
duchess
thirsty
murderers
impatient
strumpets
horrible
beautiful creatures
proposed
concert
pavilion
enchanting
suffering
divine
noble

chairbearer
stricken with infirmity
he's incapable
ugliness
lackeys
appalling
rudeness
servant
prosecutor
gambling
suspending all proceedings
amiable
brocade
intolerable
monkey parrot
dazzle them with treasure

imprisoned
luxury
creditors
banish this nightmare
compliments
hesitate
journey
bewitched
poison
grovel on the ground
despicable
resemble
repulsive

Before the Movie

1. Based on fairy tales you have heard, what are some themes you expect to see in the film?

2. Write a brief outline of main events you expect to see in the story.

During the Movie

1. Compare events in the story as they unfold with the outlines made before the movie.

2. Describe the father. What drove him to enter the Beast's castle?

3. How do you think Beauty's father felt about his daughter taking his place at the castle?

After the Movie

1. In what ways was the Beast human? How was he an animal?

2. What moral message can you derive from this story?

3. What do you think happened to Beauty's sisters and brother?

4. The opera *La Belle et la Bête* was written by Philip Glass to accompany the film. You can turn down the sound from the film and replace it with the music from Glass's opera. This opera is synchronized with the plot. It would be interesting to play the movie, or clips of the movie, twice to determine the effects of the opera on general enjoyment and understanding. (If your students enjoy the operatic version of *Beauty and the*

Beast, you might want to show *Umbrellas of Cherbourg*, another musical film.)

Language Arts Activities

To set the mood, play Wagner's *Tristan und Isolde* while students are engaged in the activities.

1. Beauty and the Beast parallels, to some extent, Cinderella. After reading Cinderella, compare Cinderella's life with Beauty's. What are some of the underlying themes common to both stories (e.g., greed, envy, industry, love)? (language arts standard 2)

2. Compare different versions of *Beauty and the Beast* (see Related Resources). Analyze each of the parts of the story grammar: introduction, characters, setting, rising and falling action, climax, and dénouement (solution) and determine similarities and differences. A Venn diagram is one way to record information. (language arts standards 1 and 3)

3. Make a list of material goods and behaviors that are real (fact) or made up (fiction). Relate your list to the opening prologue of the film, which states that little children are accepting of things impossible. (language arts standard 2)

4. The words "Once upon a time" create memories and fond expectations of the story to come. Create an individual or group story beginning with "Once upon a time" to tell to young children. Combine elements of fact and fiction in your story. (language arts standards 1, 3, and 6)

5. Create a character for one of the human candleholders seen in the Beast's castle. Provide a personal description, background, and human interest story for your human candleholder. Base your descriptions on the culture of 18th-century France. (language arts standards 6 and 7)

6. Read a variety of folk tales from France. Share folk tales through drama, art, and puppetry. (language arts standards 1, 2, 4, and 6)

7. After reading a variety of folk tales from France, compare the dominant themes from each. Using a Venn diagram, analyze and record similarities and

differences between a selected folk tale and *Beauty and the Beast*. (language arts standard 6)

Social Studies Activities

1. Make a list of turning points in the lives of Beauty, the Beast, and Beauty's father. Describe how each of these defining moments impacted their lives and the lives of others. (social studies standard V)

2. Create a map of France that includes a small fictitious town, a seaport, and a rural location for the Beast's mansion. Using clues from the film, including terrain and the time required to travel distances, determine how far apart to place each of the areas on the map. What large French cities and geographic landforms are closest to your fictitious areas? (social studies standard III)

3. Create a modern-day setting for the story. How would cultural influences of family, religion, and socioeconomic status impact the setting? (social studies standards III and V)

4. The Beast used human forms as grotesque candleholders. What rights, if any, would protect these human candleholders from exploitation or abuse in 18th-century France? Compare the rights of people in 18th-century France with rights of people today. (social studies standard VI)

Related Resources

Fiction

The Rose and the Beast: Fairy Tales Retold by Francesca Lia Block
Tale of Despereaux: Being the Story of a Mouse, a Princess, Some Soup, and a Spool of Thread by Kate Dicamillo
Beauty: A Retelling of the Story of Beauty and the Beast by Robin McKinley
Rose Daughter by Robin McKinley
Beast by Donna Jo Napoli
The Complete Phantom of the Opera by George Perry
The Complete Fairy Tales of Charles Perrault translated by Neil Philip

I Capture the Castle by Dodie Smith
Beauty and the Beast: And Other Classic French Fairy Tales by Jack David Zipes, editor

Music

La Belle et la Bête by Philip Glass
Tristan und Isolde by Wagner

THE BICYCLE THIEF

Grade Level: 6–12
Time: 89 minutes
Filmed: 1948 in black and white
Language: Italian
Genre: Drama
Director: Vittorio De Sica
Rating: Not rated
Theme: Every man has a breaking point.
Interesting Fact: "As though the soul of a man has been filmed." (Arthur Miller)
Setting: Rome, Italy, 1947. Two years after the end of World War II. A postwar depression has left much of Italy in poverty.

Summary

This story is about the unthinkable. A sensitive, honest family man is driven to an act of crime by life's circumstances. Worse, the man's fall from morality and the law occurs in front of his young son, stripping him at once of his dignity and sense of self-worth.

Antonio Ricci has been spending his days in employment lines alongside hundreds of other men desperate for work. His family has pawned most of its belongings, including a bicycle, to get money for food. Antonio is finally offered a job hanging posters, on the condition that he has a bicycle. He accepts the job, and through the sacrifices of his family, reclaims his bicycle from the pawnshop.

The bicycle represents Antonio's only means of providing for his family. When his bicycle is stolen, Antonio and his son begin a frantic search for the thief through the streets of Rome. Antonio eventually encounters the thief, but the thief has already disposed of the bicycle, probably selling it for parts. With every hope dashed, in an agonizing moment of conscience and need, Antonio makes a choice that ends in humiliation and anguish for both father and son.

Characters

Antonio Ricci: An out-of-work family man who finds a job that requires a bicycle.
Maria Ricci: Antonio's supportive wife and the mother of Bruno.
Bruno: The young son of Antonio and Maria who helps his father look for his bicycle.
Santona: "Religious" psychic from whom the Riccis seek help. They get none.
Alfredo: The bicycle thief.
Biacco: A friend who tries to help find the bicycle.

Outline of Events

1. A mass of people are in line at an employment office. Employment agencies have far more applicants than jobs; the population is desperate to find work. Antonio Ricci is singled out of the crowd and offered a job if he has a bicycle. He does not, but he accepts the job anyway.

2. Antonio goes home to his wife, Maria, and tells her his plight about needing a bicycle for his new job. He feels sorry for himself, saying, "I've been cursed since the day I was born. I feel like a man in chains." Antonio's helpless attitude renders him incapable of taking positive action to reclaim his bicycle from the pawnshop.

3. Maria strips their beds, proclaiming, "We don't need sheets to sleep," and sells them at a pawnshop to get money to redeem Antonio's pawned bicycle. It is obvious that other families are equally desperate; the pawnshop is filled with belongings once considered necessities but now pawned to raise money for the bare necessities of life. Maria asks her husband whether they can run an errand; he finds out she is going to see Santona, the psychic, and admonishes her for spending money foolishly.

4. During Antonio's first day on the job, while on a ladder hanging posters, his bicycle is stolen. Antonio chases the thief but cannot catch him. When he goes to the police, they are indifferent, offering him little help. Antonio realizes that he must find the thief on his own.

5. The next day Antonio, his friend Biacco, and Bruno look for the stolen bicycle at bicycle markets, where bicycles are often sold for parts. There are literally thousands of bicycles and even more parts, so they have no luck. They try a second market, but it starts to rain and everyone begins to leave. While Antonio and Bruno take shelter under the eaves of a building, Antonio sees the bicycle thief speaking to an old man. Antonio and Bruno run after them, catching up with the old man. The old man does not want to talk to Antonio and goes into a mission serving soup to street people. Antonio follows him into a church service, where he threatens the old man with jail. The old man runs from the church. The parishioners block Antonio, thinking he is accosting the old man, and the old man gets away.

6. Antonio tells Bruno to wait by a bridge while he gives chase to the old man. During the chase Antonio hears frantic calls for someone to help a drowning boy. Certain that it is Bruno, Antonio runs to the scene. A boy is carried out of the water and to Antonio's intense relief it is not Bruno. He looks around and sees Bruno patiently waiting for him. Emotionally drained, wet, and hungry, Antonio and Bruno take a break for food and wine. Refreshed, Antonio begins dreaming of the money he can make by hanging posters, which inspires him to look even harder for his bicycle. Desperate to find his bicycle, he seeks council from Santona, the psychic, who tells him that if he does not find the bicycle that day, he won't find it at all.

7. As he is leaving Santona's building, Antonio once again sees the thief. After a chase he confronts him. The thief, Alfredo, supported by a gang of neighbors, denies everything. During the chaos, Alfredo has a seizure. Bruno, seeing a policeman, brings him to Alfredo. Together they search Alfredo's home and find no evidence against him. Antonio learns that with no witnesses or evidence, he has no case against Alfredo.

8. After two days of searching with his young son, Bruno, Antonio realizes that finding his bike is hopeless. In a city where thousands of people

own bicycles, Antonio's hunt for one particular bicycle is like hunting for a needle in a haystack.

9. Dejected, Antonio stares at hundreds of bicycles parked by a soccer stadium. One bicycle in particular is isolated from the rest and is seemingly unguarded. Antonio is at his wit's end; he is desperate to get a bicycle. He sends his son, Bruno, to catch a streetcar home, knowing that he is about to stoop to stealing. In his frenzied state he steals the unguarded bicycle, unaware that his son is still nearby.

10. Antonio is quickly caught and the authorities move to arrest him. Antonio is taunted and shamed in front of his son. The owner of the bicycle, seeing the confused and hurt look in Bruno's eyes, decides not to press charges, saying that Antonio has enough problems. Antonio breaks down and walks away with Bruno, hand in hand, morally destitute.

Vocabulary

A lengthy list of words and phrases from the subtitles of this film is provided. From this list teachers can choose the words most appropriate for their classes. Words appear in chronological order so they may be introduced and reviewed as needed.

deaf
difficult
bricklayer
thief
employment office
excuse me
work permit
urgent
rotten luck
barber
liner and cotton
obliged
storeroom
grateful
autumn
pasta and potatoes
lire (currency)
disgraceful
predicted
drowning
stupidity
jacket
omelet
mozzarella
inspector
million
intelligent
soccer
license plate
understand

Department of Labor
sued for libel
welfare check
sued for slander
humiliates workers
witnesses
rehearsing
innocent
vegetables
streetcar
whistle
criminal
celebrate
scoundrel
serial number
arrested
mistakes

Before the Movie

1. Think about the things you own. What possession is most essential to your well-being?

2. If you lost your most prized possession, to what lengths would you go to find it?

During the Movie

1. How are Antonio and his family affected by the postwar depression?

2. What do you think contributed to the postwar depression that left Italy in poverty?

3. How are the people in Rome coping with poverty?

After the Movie

1. What is the main emotion you are feeling after watching this movie?

2. What was Antonio searching for besides a bicycle?

3. Is this a realistic film? Why or why not?

4. Look at the movie through the son's eyes. How do you think he feels about his father? How do you think the relationship between father and son will be changed?

5. To what extent did the fact that Antonio was a victim of theft make him more likely to be a perpetrator of theft? That is, did the theft of Antonio's bicycle make him more likely, in turn, to steal a bicycle?

Language Arts Activities

1. Write a summary of the story through Bruno's eyes. (language arts standards 5 and 6)

2. A famous playwright, Arthur Miller, describing the complexities of the main character said, "As though the soul of a man has been filmed." Examine the life and actions of Antonio. Make a list of traits you think best describe his character. Write a description of the soul of Antonio. Compare descriptions and discuss. (language arts standards 3 and 5)

3. If you must have a job to support yourself and you need a car to keep your job, make a list of items you would be willing to sell to get money for a car. What other means could you use to earn money for a car? (language arts standards 3, 5, and 6)

4. Make a chart with three sections. In each section write how war affected the lives of men, women, and children in the film. (language arts standard 3)

5. Research the economy of postwar Italy. What problems did the citizens face in their day-to-day lives? Brainstorm some possible solutions to the problems you found. Working independently or in small groups, choose a problem and write a report stating the background, questions explored, and recommendations. (language arts standards 5 and 7)

Social Studies Activities

1. Divide students into two groups. Read about the efforts of the United States, through the Marshall Plan, to help nations in western Europe reduce extreme poverty and help rebuild their infrastructure. Debate for and against the Marshall Plan. Through research, one group determines reasons America should not have engaged in nation building by supporting the Marshall Plan; the other group determines reasons America should have engaged in nation building by supporting the Marshall Plan. (social studies standard VI)

2. Why were bicycles valuable enough to steal? Think about the effects of supply and demand. What causes goods to rise or fall in value? Consider how personal and cultural values influenced the actions of Antonio Ricci. (social studies standard VII)

3. The story took place in 1947 when postwar unemployment was rampant. If you were a politician in Italy during the postwar depression, what plan would you develop for American aid? Describe the difficulties of getting American aid to those who really need it. (social studies standard VII)

4. Analyze citizens' rights and responsibilities. What rights did Antonio have? How were his rights violated? What role did the actions of others have on the dignity of Antonio? If the rule of law had been followed, what would the course of events have been for Antonio? In your mind, was justice served? (social studies standard X)

Related Resources

Fiction

Presumption of Guilt by Jeffrey Ashford
Crime and Punishment by Fyodor Dostoyevsky

Nonfiction

The Marshall Plan by Allen W. Dulles
The Marshall Plan: America, Britain, and the Reconstruction of Western Europe by Michael J. Hogan

CHILDREN OF HEAVEN

Grade Level: 6–12
Filmed: 1997 in color
Genre: Drama
Rating: PG
Time: 83 minutes
Language: Persian
Director: Majid Majidi
Theme: Little mistakes have consequences that expand with time.
Interesting Fact: This movie won the Grand Prix du Americas at the Montreal Film Festival in 1997 but was not released in the United States until 1999.
Setting: Modern-day Tehran, the capital city of Iran. It is the cultural and economic center of the country and the most populated city in Iran.

Summary

Many Iranian children live in poverty; one pair of shoes is considered plenty for each child at school. The story is shown from the viewpoint of two young children, Ali, a nine-year-old boy, and Zahra, his seven-year-old sister. Their mother has back problems and must rest, while their father struggles to make a living to support his family.

Though Ali Mandegar and his sister Zahra live in the Middle East during times of political turmoil, their immediate worries are not concerns of the world but of the moment: how to go to school sharing a single pair of shoes.

After the loss of Zahra's shoes, Ali and Zahra, by sharing Ali's sneakers, weave a beautiful tale as they cope with their family's poverty while supporting each other. Throughout the story, Ali tries to think of ways to get a new pair of shoes for his sister. His final plan demonstrates the great lengths he will go to rectify his mistake of losing Zahra's shoes. Ali goes the extra mile in an attempt to win a pair of shoes for his sister. Viewers will be cheering, but not too hard, for Ali at the end of the movie.

Characters

Ali Mandegar: A nine-year-old boy in the third grade. He accidentally loses his sister's shoes and offers to share his until her shoes can be found.

Zahra Mandegar: Little sister to Ali. She supports Ali by keeping the lost shoes a secret from their impoverished family.

Mother: Mother to Ali, Zahra, and another baby. She is an invalid.

Father: A hardworking, honest man trying to support his family.

Mr. Jafari: Ali's teacher who believes in his potential.

School principal: Stern administrator who catches Ali arriving at school late and threatens to expel him for his tardiness.

Trashman: Unwittingly picks up a bag containing Zahra's shoes. Thinking they have been discarded, he sells them.

Roya: A girl in Zahra's class who unknowingly wears Zahra's shoes, which her father bought from the trashman.

Coach: Gives Ali a chance to run in the race.

Outline of Events

1. Because Ali's mother is an invalid, it is his job to run the errands. He picks up his sister's shoes from the shoe repair shop and stops at the vegetable stand to buy food for his mother. Ali sets down the shoes while selecting produce, and a man collecting trash mistakenly picks up the shoes.

2. Ali must go home and tell his sister what happened. He explains to Zahra, through tears, that he lost her shoes. The two discuss the family finances, realizing that buying Zahra another pair of shoes is not feasible.

3. With a sick mother and an overworked father, Ali and Zahra must help with the chores at home. The father, while scolding Ali for not doing enough to help his mother, says, "You are not a kid anymore. You're nine years old."

4. Ali and Zahra have worked out a plan to share shoes. Zahra goes to school first and wears Ali's "ugly" sneakers. She must race to meet Ali to give him the shoes so he can go to school. Ali gets in trouble by arriving to school late, but the secret of the lost shoes must be kept from his parents at all costs.

5. Ali wins a beautiful pen for earning good grades at school and gives it to his sister, trying to compensate for losing her shoes. The next day Zahra spots Roya, a girl at school, wearing her shoes. Roya's father bought the shoes from the trashman for his daughter. When Ali and Zahra follow Roya to her house, they see her father is blind and quietly leave.

6. While serving tea at a mourning ceremony at the mosque, Ali's father is given some gardening tools. Elated, he takes Ali into a wealthy part of town to seek work. After several rejections they finally find someone who needs their services. The father is well paid; he leaves with dreams of earning more money as a gardener.

7. Zahra loses the pen Ali has given her, but it is found and returned by Roya. During this exchange, Zahra sees that Roya has new shoes and wonders where her old ones are. Zahra's shoes are once again with the trashman.

8. Ali finally sees a way to right the shoe situation when he hears of a boys' race; the third prize is a pair of sneakers! With much coaxing, the

coach allows Ali to enter the race as a representative from his school. With thoughts of his sister, he runs with all his heart, ruining his own shoes. Dismayed, he learns he won first place, not the needed third place that would earn him shoes as a prize.

9. After the race there is a touching scene between Ali and his sister when she sees he did not win the pair of sneakers. Now they have no shoes. However, while Ali is soaking his blistered feet and Zahra is once again helping her mother, their father is at the market, his bicycle loaded with food and two pairs of new shoes.

Vocabulary

A lengthy list of words and phrases from the subtitles of this film is provided. From this list teachers can choose the words most appropriate for their classes. Words appear in chronological order so they may be introduced and reviewed as needed.

toumans (currency)
permission sir
potatoes
offering stew
account has reached its limit
obedient to the teacher
disappeared
organize your time
collapse
check fingernails regularly
laundry
bacteria
destroying
irresponsible student
repaired
spraying trees
teasing me
plowing the garden
shoes disappeared
equipment
tomorrow
fertilizer
pain in the neck
vacation
mourning ceremony
neighborhood
landlord
motorcycle
heavy
brakes are gone
sugar
hold on tight
mosque
insolent man
coupons
idiot

grocer
empty-handed
slipped disc
attention students
surgery
long-distance races
forbidden slippers
province
crippled
register
sneakers
preliminary selection
unfortunately
protesting
go to practice
with permission
vegetables
deadline
gutter
pigheaded
wait a minute
four kilometers
shallow
sportsmanship

Before the Movie

1. Write a brief description of what you think life is like in Iran for an average family.

2. How many pairs of shoes do you have? How many do you really need?

3. Think of a time you lost something that belonged to another person. What did you do?

4. What do you think Iranian students do at school? How do you think life in Iranian schools compares with life in your school?

During the Movie

1. Notice all of the people keep their shoes outside the house. Why do you think they do that? Is that a part of their culture? Do people in other cultures take off their shoes before entering the house?

2. What do the shoes represent to Ali and Zahra?

3. Imagine if you had to share a pair of shoes. How would that affect your life?

After the Movie

1. Compare the description you wrote about life in Iran before you saw the film with what you have learned after viewing the film.

2. Was the race for more than just a pair of shoes? What do you think it meant for Ali?

3. Think about Ali and Zahra's neighborhood and home. How do their living conditions and customs compare with yours?

4. What universal behaviors were exhibited before, during, and after the race?

5. The father is hardworking and honest. Cite specific instances that support this description.

Language Arts Activities

1. As seen in the film, Iranian students—boys and girls—wear uniforms to school. Research the types of uniforms worn in American schools. Compare Iranian and American school uniforms. Discuss reasons for school uniforms in American and Iranian schools. Are the reasons different or similar? Draw and describe the uniform you would require if you ran a school. (language arts standards 2, 3, 7, and 8)

2. Find recent news coverage on Iran and other countries in the Middle East. Work in groups to write and produce a newscast that features the lost shoes. Tie in the story of the lost shoes with current events. (language arts standards 4, 5, 7, and 8)

3. Write a story from the shoes' point of view. Base the story on places and events in the film. (language arts standards 5 and 6)

4. Using a concept map, write "Lost Shoes" in a circle. Draw spokes that radiate from the center. On each spoke, write a consequence that resulted from the lost shoes. (language arts standard 3)

5. Using the scaled map from the first social studies activity on the following page, write a description of the route from your house to your

school. Have a partner read and critique your description to determine clarity and accuracy. (language arts standard 5)

Social Studies Activities

1. Think about Ali having to learn the way to school, the market, and back home again. After determining or estimating distances, create a scaled map from your house to your school. (social studies standard III)

2. The setting of the story is in Tehran, the capital city of Iran. Study the topography of Iran and determine why Tehran was selected as the capital. Consider physical features and climate. Look for other places in Iran that might be more suitable for a capital city. This activity can be extended to other countries in the Middle East. (social studies standard III)

3. Look at a map of Iran. Based on the latitude, make a list of agricultural products you think could be grown in Iran. Look at the topography, including rivers and other bodies of water. How do you think products are transported throughout the country? (social studies standards III and VII)

4. Create a timeline of the lost shoes. Begin with manufacturing and distribution of the shoes, then record the events in the film. (social studies standard VII)

5. Ali's father was responsible for supporting his family. Discuss the responsibilities you have as a member of a family, as a student, and as a citizen. (social studies standards I, IV, and X)

Related Resources

Fiction

Persian Cinderella Story by Shirley Climo

Nonfiction

Dropping in on Iran by Philip Bader and Patricia Moritz
A Taste of Persia: An Introduction to Persian Cooking by Najmieh Batmanglij

Modern Iran: Roots and Results of a Revolution by Nikki R. Keddie
Iran the Beautiful by Daniel Nadler
Iran (Countries: Faces and Places) by Elma Schemenauer

CROUCHING TIGER, HIDDEN DRAGON

Grade Level: 9–12
Filmed: 2000 in color
Genre: Fantasy, action
Rating: PG-13
Time: 120 minutes
Language: Mandarin
Director: Ang Lee
Theme: Sacrifice by good people is always necessary to overcome evil.
Interesting Fact: The fighting special effects were created by cinematographer Yuen Woo Ping, who also is repsonsible for the fighting special effects in *The Matrix*.
Setting: Nineteenth-century China, in and around Peking during the latter part of the Ch'ing (Qing) Dynasty.

Summary

This movie belongs to a fantasy genre in Chinese literature and film called wuxia. Wuxia chronicles the stories of martial arts warriors who possess superhuman qualities, including the ability to defy gravity.

Ownership of the Green Destiny sword is the focus of this award-winning martial arts film. Li Mu Bai and Shu Lien, honorable warriors, compete for the Green Destiny with marauding gang members. The importance of the sword lies in its magical powers of speed and deft movement.

Two love stories intertwined with nonstop action provide the pathos and interest that hold the plot of the film together. A surprise element is the resolve and fighting prowess of the lead women, Jade Fox, Jen, and Shu Lien. These women break the social norms of subservience to men and arranged marriages to seek their own destinies and to be "true to themselves."

At its core, this is a story about Jen's quest for power and love, Li Mu Bai's journey toward peace, Shu Lien's love for Li Mu Bai, and Lo's longing for Jen. Sadly, the search for Jen and the Green Destiny sword ends with loss of life.

In addition to a vivid cinematic depiction of China, this movie provides a discussion for gender roles and the importance of honor and responsibility. Finally, it should be noted that a flashback scene is inserted midway through the movie. This provides an opportunity to discuss critical events leading up to the flashback.

Characters

Yu Shu Lien: Female warrior in love with Li Mu Bai but has kept secret her affections for him.

Li Mu Bai: Wudan warrior hero who gives up his sword to pursue a more fulfilling life.

Jen Yu: Young aristocrat who secretly possesses superior martial arts skills but is bound to an aristocratic life. She longs for adventure.

Lo (Dark Cloud): Desert renegade who ambushes the Yu family's caravan en route to Peking and falls in love with Jen.

Jade Fox: Known criminal who is distrustful of men. She stole a Wudan martial arts manual to secretly train Jen in its methods.

Sir Te: Friend of Li Mu Bai and Shu Lien and guardian of the Green Destiny after it is given to him by Li Mu Bai.

Yun Fat: Master of Li Mu Bai.

Outline of Events

1. Wanting to abandon his warrior life, Li Mu Bai asks Shu Lien to deliver the Green Destiny sword as a gift to a friend, Sir Te. Master Li claims the sword "brought him as much trouble as glory."

2. A masked person arrives and steals the sword from its new guardian, claiming that the sword represents freedom. Jade Fox, an enemy of Li Mu Bai, joins in the fight to help the thief. During the fight Li Mu Bai yells, "The fox is out of her hole." The fight that ensues between Jade Fox and Li Mu Bai is to avenge the death of Li Mu Bai's master, Yun Fat.

3. Li Mu Bai tries to convert Jen, Jade Fox's assistant, into an honorable warrior. She deceives him into thinking she is considering his words, then viciously turns on him, using the Green Destiny. Without the sword, Jen returns to her quarters, where she is reacquainted with Lo, the young renegade she met in the desert when her family was ambushed.

4. In a lengthy flashback sequence, Jen's family is shown being ambushed by desert renegades. Jen falls in love with Lo, head of the Dark Cloud gang of bandits, during a long pursuit to retrieve a comb that Lo has stolen. Although Jen gets the comb back from Lo, she remains with him in his hideout. When a search party for Jen nears the renegades' encampment, she leaves and gives the comb back to Lo, with the promise that they will be together again. She wants to stay with Lo, but he tells her to consider all she would leave behind. To stay, Jen must give up her parents and her comfortable way of life.

5. Jen returns to Peking where she marries in a traditional Chinese wedding ceremony. The viewer is treated only to the initial scenes where Jen is riding in a grand procession to the wedding ceremony. During this time, Lo and his gang ride in and try to stop the wedding. They are beaten back, and Jen marries.

6. In another love story, Shu Lien and Li Mu Bai fall in love as they seek the Green Destiny sword. In a touching scene, Li looks at Shu Lien's hands, saying, "Your hands are rough and calloused." He takes her hand, and they profess their love for one another.

7. By nightfall, Jen is missing, as well as the Green Destiny sword. Eventually Li Mu Bai is able to find her, but when he throws the Green Destiny into a waterfall, Jen lunges after it, only to be swooped up by Jade Fox. Miraculously, Jen recovers the sword and holds tight to it during the time she thinks she is being nursed back to health by Jade Fox.

8. When Li Mu Bai finds Jen again, she is alone in a cave. He sees that Jade Fox has drugged her. Shu Lien follows Jade Fox into the cave and arrives just at the moment when Jade Fox is attacking Li Mu Bai with poisoned pins.

9. Jade Fox is overcome and dies, but one of the poisoned pins has pierced Li Mu Bai. Jen knows the antidote but cannot get it soon enough to save Li Mu Bai. He dies in the arms of Shu Lien, where, with his last breath, he professes his love for her. Shu Lien sends Jen to Wudan Mountain to join Lo, telling her, "Be true to yourself."

10. In the morning at Wudan Mountain, Jen jumps off the side of a brick wall into the water below to demonstrate a proverb that says "a faithful heart makes wishes come true."

Vocabulary

A lengthy list of words and phrases from the subtitles of this film is provided. From this list teachers can choose the words most appropriate for their classes. Words appear in chronological order so they may be introduced and reviewed as needed.

business
exquisite
deep meditation
machete
silence
congratulatory
surrounding
manipulative
enlightened
Imperial Court
endless sorrow
royalty
convoy
official
Green Destiny
Royal Guard
Peking
West (western China)
murder
governess
governor
silk pajamas
personal

consortium
weapon
Dark Cloud
custodian
Manchurian
daughter
orphan
coy
desert
wasting precious time
defeated foe
cowards
amazing technique
idiot
invincible
earful
poisoned needle
weapons
antidote
scabbard
antithesis
beautiful, but dangerous
meditate

Before the Movie

Note: Because of the unfamiliar spelling of Chinese names, it would be helpful to list and review the names before showing the film. To demystify the names, provide students with a list of the characters.

1. This film is about a magical sword, the Green Destiny. If you had a magical sword, how would you use it?

2. Look for elements of fantasy during the story.

3. Think of a time when you or someone close to you acted in revenge. What string of events occurred as a direct result of the revenge? Look for the part of the plot that deals with revenge and keep in mind its consequences.

During the Movie

1. The movie depicts a woman who does not want to lead the life her family has arranged for her. What do you think was the typical role of a woman at this time?

2. Which character do you most admire and why?

After the Movie

1. What were some of the significant events that occurred after the sword was stolen?

2. Which action scenes added the most interest to the story? Did any of the action scenes detract from the story?

3. What role did revenge play in the story?

Language Arts Activities

1. Wuxia is a genre of film and literature that chronicles martial arts warriors with superhuman strengths and abilities. What specific scenes would classify this movie as a wuxia genre film? (language arts standard 2)

2. During the Ch'ing Dynasty (1644–1911), women were subservient to men and expected to remain in their homes. Because females were not valued, many female babies were neglected or killed. Read about life during the Ch'ing Dynasty. Determine how the roles of the women in the story differ from women who lived during the Ch'ing Dynasty. What commonalities do you see between the two groups of women? (language arts standards 1, 7, and 8)

3. Compare the roles of women who lived during the Ch'ing Dynasty with women today. (language arts standard 1)

4. View pictures and drawings of the Ch'ing Dynasty. Determine aspects of their culture including dress, recreation, art, social interactions, and celebrations. Create a poster or painting depicting cultural traditions during the Ch'ing Dynasty. (language arts standard 7)

5. The name *Ch'ing* means pure. Read about the Ch'ing Dynasty to determine ways it lived up to the meaning of its name. Rename the Ch'ing Dynasty using a synonym for pure. Write a brief description of your renamed dynasty, stating its methods and goals. (language arts standards 1, 2, and 5)

Social Studies Activities

1. China has a rich cultural history that promoted the development of dynasties. This movie took place during the Ch'ing Dynasty, the last of the dynasties, which lasted about 250 years from 1644 to 1911. Based on the film, make a list of traditions and aspects of its culture. Interpret the culture of the Ch'ing Dynasty from the perspective of life today. Note similarities and differences. (social studies standard II)

2. For over 2,000 years, China was a monarchy. The Ch'ing Dynasty was overthrown in 1911 and replaced by a republican form of government. Later, after World War II, tremendous battles occurred between the Nationalists and the Communists. Make a timeline showing the ruling factions in China after the fall of the Ch'ing Dynasty. (social studies standard VI)

3. At the beginning of the Han Dynasty (about A.D. 920), the Chinese began the cultural tradition of binding female babies' feet; small feet

represented a sign of beauty. This tradition lasted until the end of the imperial dynasties and was banned by the new Chinese republic in 1911. Compare foot binding with customs today related to beauty and aesthetics. (social studies standards I and IV)

Related Resources

Fiction

Tales From China (Oxford Myths and Legends) by Cyril Birch
The Good Earth by Pearl S. Buck
The Blue Lotus by Hergé
The Legend of Mu Lan: A Heroine of Ancient China by Wei Jiang
The Hero and the Crown by Robin McKinley
The Thief by Megan Whalen Turner
I Rode a Horse of Milk White Jade by Diane Lee Wilson

Nonfiction

Science in Ancient China by George W. Beshore
Eyewitness: Ancient China by Arthur Cotterell
Pageant of Chinese History by Elizabeth Seeger
Made in China: Ideas and Inventions From Ancient China by Suzanne Williams and Andrea Fong
Chinese Cinderella: The True Story of an Unwanted Daughter by Adeline Yen Mah

THE CUP

Grade Level: 6–12
Filmed: 1999 in color
Genre: Drama
Rating: G
Time: 94 minutes
Language: Bhutanese
Director: Khyentse Norbu
Theme: Instantaneous communication drastically shrinks the effective distance among people, reducing differences in culture.

Interesting Facts: The male lead, Geko, was played by the real Orgyen, the young monk featured in the film. The director, Khyentse Norbu is, himself, a Bhutanese Holy Man.
Setting: A Tibetan monastery in India in 1998.

Summary

"Inevitable modernization comes from the ideas of the young." This quote from the film epitomizes the film's plot. Older monks live their lives based on traditions of the past, established by years of prayerful solitude. Each group of entering young student monks brings with it an element of change based on youthful exuberance and knowledge of the outside world they just left.

This story recounts how one spirited student monk, Orgyen, with a dream of seeing the 1998 World Cup football (soccer) game between France and Italy, was able to lead the other student monks into helping him fulfill his dream. More important, he was able to convince the older monks—who had little or no understanding of what he was proposing—to support him.

Orgyen wants to see the World Cup games and convinces the other student monks to sneak out at night and go into town to watch a semifinal football (soccer) game on television. They are caught by Geko, their superior, when they try to sneak back into the monastery. Geko reluctantly tells the abbot. The kindly abbot does not punish the new student monks but assigns the others to kitchen duty as punishment.

Orgyen devises a plan to bring the final game of the World Cup to the monastery. Though the young student monks know a little about football (soccer), having played a crude game of football with a can during their recreational time, they are not all as enthusiastic as Orgyen. He convinces his friends to donate money to rent a TV. To pay for a surprise price increase, one of the newest monks, Nyima, reluctantly parts with a watch his mother gave him. In the end, all the monks enjoy the game except Orgyen. He is overwhelmed with guilt for having put the new monk's most prized possession at risk. The gentle teachings of Buddhism are seen throughout the film, especially at the end.

Characters

Geko: Older monk in charge of the young student monks.
Orgyen: Impetuous newly ordained young monk. He is the leader of the young monks. He schemes to bring a TV to the monastery.
The abbot: Head of the monastery. Exiled to India, he constantly dreams of returning to Tibet.
Nyima: Young boy just entering the monastery. He is the homesick nephew of Palden.
Palden: One of the two new monks who arrived from Nepal. He is the uncle of Nyima.
The predictor: Older resident of the monastery. Presumably he has the power of seeing the future.
The Indian: Merchant who rents TVs and satellite dishes for a living.

Outline of Events

1. The opening scenes show lengthy ceremonies dating back 2,500 years by the monks and monks in training. Though the viewer is introduced to all the major characters, the story is slowly paced, initially.

2. The monks at the monastery are in exile from Tibet, ruled by China. Two new boys are expected to arrive at the monastery from Nepal. The elder monks are concerned, thinking the new boys had problems crossing the border from Nepal into India. Political and natural obstacles pose a danger to them. When they finally arrive, they say they had problems crossing the border, but few details are given.

3. One of the young boys, Nyima, has a watch, given to him by his mother. He is homesick but says he has no home to return to.

4. The young monks-in-training enjoy playing games, including kicking a can around the grounds in a crudely played game of football (soccer). One night, they sneak away from the monastery to go into the village to see the semifinal game of the 1998 World Cup between France and Italy. During the game, Orgyen explains the game to his fellow monks. This irritates people sitting nearby, and they are thrown out. When they protest that they paid money to see the game, the proprietor refunds their

money by throwing it on the ground. Upset they didn't get to see the soccer game, the young monks hope they can at least return to the monastery undetected by the senior monks. Unfortunately, their bad luck continues; Geko, the monk in charge of the student monks, sees them.

5. Geko must report the misdeeds of the student monks to the Abbot. The Abbot, not knowing about the World Cup, becomes preoccupied, not by the behavior of the boys, but with the World Cup. He asks Geko to explain the World Cup to him. Geko tells him, "Two civilized nations are fighting over a ball." Incredulous, the Abbot asks Geko if he is joking. The Abbot asks whether violence or sex is involved. Geko replies there is sometimes violence, but no sex. To punish the monks for sneaking away from the monastery, the Abbot tells Geko that the new monks are excused, but the older student monks must do the cooking.

6. The young monks scheme to get a TV to watch the final game of the World Cup between France and Brazil at the monastery. They ask Geko for permission to raise money to rent a TV so they can watch the game. They promise him that if they can watch the World Cup, they will study harder and not skip classes. They propose their picnic day be replaced by a night of TV. When asked where they will get the TV, Orgyen replies that they can rent a TV from an "Indian guy."

7. Geko goes to the abbot to ask permission. The abbot, seen continually packing his belongings in hopes of returning to Tibet someday, gives permission. When Geko tells him the game is shown at midnight, the abbot, showing a total lack of awareness of time zones, replies that midnight is a strange time to play a game. He asks what the winner gets and is puzzled when he is told the winner gets a cup. The abbot looks at the cup he is holding, probably wondering why two nations would care about winning a cup!

8. The World Cup is to be broadcast at midnight. The young monks have just a few hours to raise 300 rupees to rent a TV and a satellite dish. The young monks contribute their own money and then run from room to room asking the older monks for money. They generously donate their money, and the 300 rupees are raised. However, when the young monks go to the

Indian to rent the equipment, he tells them the price is higher during the time of the World Cup. The boys must raise an additional 50 rupees for a black and white TV and 100 rupees for color. Having exhausted all sources of money, Orgyen tells Palden that since he is Nyima's uncle, he should ask Nyima to give them his watch to make up the additional money owed the Indian. Orgyen gives Palden his solemn word that he will get Nyima's watch back from the Indian.

9. With the donation of the watch, the young monks are able to rent a black-and-white TV and a satellite dish. The Indian tells Orgyen that he will sell the watch if Orgyen doesn't bring the money by noon the next day.

10. Having spent all their money on the TV and satellite dish, the young monks must set up their own equipment. The Indian, angered when the young monks don't hire him to set up the equipment, spitefully tells them to face the antenna north, the wrong direction to get reception. The young monks transport the TV and satellite dish back to the monastery on a tractor and rush to get the equipment set up by midnight.

11. The equipment is set up, and all of the monks are assembled to watch the game. They consider the direction the sun rises to determine where to point the satellite. Following the Indian's directions of pointing the antenna north, they are unable to get a picture. In desperation they rotate the satellite dish to the south and are able to see their game. Just as they begin watching the game, the electricity goes off. One young monk wishes he lived in a more civilized country. The young monks bring in a lantern and begin making shadow puppets and telling stories.

12. The power is restored, and the monks are able to watch the game. Orgyen, seeing that Nyima is very upset about his watch, is overcome with worry that the Indian will sell it. He leaves the room. The abbot notices that Orgyen is missing and sends Geko to find him. Geko goes to Orgyen's room and finds him sorting through his personal belongings. Orgyen has his new pair of football (soccer) shoes sitting on his bed, thinking he can trade his shoes for the watch. Geko, taking pity on Orgyen, promises that he and the abbot will pay the additional money. During this time, France wins the World Cup. Actual footage from the World Cup game is shown.

13. Life returns to normal. The young monks are back in school. The following is an example of one of their lessons based on the teachings of Buddha:

> Can we cover earth in leather so it's soft wherever we go?
> No.
> So what can we do?
> Cover our feet in leather?
> Yes, covering our feet in leather is equal to covering the earth in leather.
> Likewise, enemies are as limitless as space.
> All enemies cannot possibly be overcome;
> All enemies cannot possibly be overcome.
> Yet if one can just overcome hatred, this will be equal to overcoming all enemies.
> All that is unsatisfactory in this world;
> All the fears and suffering that exist
> Clinging to the "I" has created it.
> What am I to do with this great demon?
> To release myself from harm and to free all others from their suffering.
> Let me give myself away and love others as I love myself.
> If a problem can be solved, why be unhappy?
> And if it cannot be solved, what is the use of being unhappy?

Epilogue:

> The story is inspired by true events. The abbot returned to Tibet. Orgyen dreams about forming the first national Tibetan football team. Many monks await the next World Cup. The Chinese are still serving rice in Tibet.

Vocabulary

A lengthy list of words and phrases from the subtitles of this film is provided. From this list teachers can choose the words most appropriate for their classes. Words appear in chronological order so they may be introduced and reviewed as needed.

crime to possess a photo
pet rabbit
monastery
daydreaming
devotion
homesick
border
washing powder
powerless
prediction

football
he's a loony
semifinals
vegetables
exiles
luggage
buildings hundreds of stories high
abbot
attachment to my homeland
journey
midnight
Nepalese border guard
permission
uprising
collecting money
study Buddhism
generous
dense population
two hundred
ordination
rascal
bribing a referee
rupees (currency)
incense
prized possession
goalkeeper
solemn word
opponent
tractor
offside
Buddha's lineage
corrupt
traditional training
incredible
modern times
threatened
precious jewel
discipline
which direction
newcomer
electricity
World Cup
nightmare
violence
scary monster
prayer flags
terrified
expelled
chaos

Before the Movie

1. What games do you like to play with your friends?

2. What is the World Cup? Have you seen the World Cup on television?

During the Movie

1. Compare the lives and living conditions of the boys in the monastery with your lives and living conditions today.

2. What is the attitude of the elder monks to the younger ones?

After the Movie

1. Why couldn't Orgyen enjoy the game?

2. How do you think it felt for the real Orgyen to star in a film about himself?

Language Arts Activities

1. Prepare an argument Orgyen can present to Geko to convince him to allow the young monks to rent a TV for the World Cup final game. (language arts standards 5 and 6)

2. Football (soccer) is the biggest sport in the world. It brings nations from all over the world together every four years to compete. Research the history of football (soccer). (language arts standards 1, 7, and 8)

3. Research accounts from the 1998 World Cup. How did the various countries involved react when their teams won or lost? Write a report describing ways the players were treated after returning home from the games. (language arts standards 1, 5, 7, 8, and 9)

4. Orgyen's dream is to establish the first national Tibetan football team. Outline a plan of action he could take to help realize his dream. Players for a country's national football team come from all over the country. Write an advertisement to attract football players to the national team. (language arts standards 5, 6, 7, and 8)

5. The following is one of the teachings from the Buddhist religion:

> Enemies are as limitless as space.
> All enemies cannot possibly be overcome.
> Yet if one can just overcome hatred, this will be equal to overcoming all enemies.

Describe how the World Cup may help conquer the hatred that leads to the creation of enemies. (language arts standards 4 and 7)

6. Throughout the movie, the student monks folded paper to make shapes relevant to their culture. This art, originated in Japan, is called

origami. Read a book on origami and create paper shapes that represent traditions stated in the film. Write a brief description or report about the shape you created. (language arts standards 2, 6, 8, and 9)

Social Studies Activities

1. Determine the history of the World Cup. When did it begin? Describe the teams that competed and list the winners. On a map, locate the countries that have participated in the World Cup. How did the 1998 World Cup contribute to the monks' global understanding of the world? (social studies standards I, III, and IX)

2. The monastery was located in India. Based on geographic clues from the movie, determine approximately where in India the monastery was located. (social studies standard III)

3. Look at a topographical map of India and the surrounding countries. Name the mountains seen in the background. (social studies standard III)

4. Compare the technology in the monastery in 1998 with technology where you live. What are the differences? What are the advantages of the technological advances we have today? Do you see any disadvantages? (social studies standard VIII)

5. Reflect on time, continuity, and change within the monastery. What was the attitude of the older monks toward the ideas of the young monks? Give examples of ways this generational gap manifests itself today. (social studies standards II and IV)

6. The abbot, reflecting the knowledge of his generation, had serious gaps in his understanding of the world based on current knowledge available today. List the statements by the abbot that indicate a lack of sophisticated knowledge about the modern world. (social studies standards II and VIII)

7. If Orgyen created a national football (soccer) team, where are the best areas for recruiting players? Read about the population distribution in India, Tibet, and Bhutan to determine where Orgyen should send his announcements advertising for players. (social studies standard III)

Related Resources

Fiction

Tintin in Tibet by Hergé

Nonfiction

Mia Hamm: On the Field With Mia Hamm by Matt Christopher
The Route to France: The World Cup 1998 by Len Coates
France and the 1998 World Cup: The National Impact of a World Sporting Event by Hugh Dauncey and Geoff Hare
The Glory Game by Hunter Davies
Our Journey From Tibet: Based on a True Story by Laurie Dolphin and Nancy Jo Johnson
Gandhi, Fighter Without a Sword by Jeanette Eaton
Soccer in Sun and Shadow by Eduardo Galeano and Mark Fried
Glenn Hoddle: The World Cup by Glenn Hoddle
World Cup France 1998: The Official Book by Keir Radnedge

DAY OF WRATH

Grade Level: 9–12
Time: 89 minutes
Filmed: 1943 in black and white
Language: Danish
Genre: Historical, witchcraft
Director: Carl Theodor Dreyer
Rating: Not rated
Theme: Good and evil are sometimes hard to distinguish.
Interesting Fact: This film was made by Theodor Dreyer in Denmark during the Nazi occupation during World War II. Dreyer had to flee to Sweden to escape Nazi internment.
Setting: Denmark in 1623, where witch trials predate the famous 1692 witchcraft trials in Salem, Massachusetts.

Summary

This film is about extremes: love and hate, natural and supernatural, life and death. The story takes place in two interrelated parts. The first part introduces Heriot's Marthe, an old peasant woman accused of witchcraft.

The second part is about Absalon, a puritanical member of the clergy who holds life and death power over women accused of being witches.

Marthe is seen giving a potion to a neighbor, saying, "There is power in evil." Is she engaging in a supernatural act, or is it simply the natural act of helping a friend? When Marthe is arrested for being a witch, she alternates between the natural, proclaiming she is not a witch, and the supernatural, where she predicts the death of others.

Absalon is experiencing grave doubts about his faith and his marriage. His thoughts are anguished. He learns that his wife not only loves his son but also despises him (Absalon) and wishes him dead. He feels guilt over sending one woman to the stake while exonerating another for personal gain. Worse, could it be that his own wife is a witch? Will she be instrumental in his death, and if so, will it be because she broke his heart, or will it be from a supernatural curse? The resulting family dynamic provides a focus on the connection of past events to the future.

This film may parallel witchcraft stories in Salem, Massachusetts, except the writers do not question whether witchcraft or witches exist. Witchcraft is simply assumed, even by those accused.

Characters

Heriot's Marthe: Old peasant woman accused of being a witch and ultimately burned at the stake.

Absalon: Older pastor married to Anne. He saved Anne's mother, an accused witch, from burning at the stake so she would allow Anne to marry him. He is a judge at the trial of Marthe.

Anne: Young daughter of a woman accused of being a witch. She is unhappily married to Absalon and in love with his son.

Martin: Absalon's son, by his first marriage. He falls in love with Anne and is pulled unwittingly toward the evils of witchcraft.

Meret: Absalon's mother. Though harsh and unlikable, she exhibits insights into everyone's motives and weaknesses.

Outline of Events

1. The story begins with two women having tea together. They hear a bell and know by the chanting that the townspeople are hunting for a witch. One of the women, Marthe, knows they are looking for her, so she sneaks out of the house.

2. Anne clashes with her mother-in-law, Meret. The mother-in-law, stern and unapproachable, clearly has no use for Anne. Absalon, seeing that his mother is hostile to his wife, is upset. However, he is overjoyed with the news that his son Martin is coming home. Joy replaces anger for the moment.

3. Martin returns, and the first person to see him is Anne. They playfully decide to play a trick on Absalon, telling him that Martin has not yet returned. Absalon, sitting at a table, sees Martin's songbook. While waiting for Martin, he reads the following from his songbook:

> **The Maiden and the Apple Tree**
> A maiden sat in an apple tree high.
> A lad chanced to pass by.
> She stretched,
> The bough it bent.
> Within his arms she landed.

During this time Martin appears and his homecoming is celebrated.

4. After Absalon and Martin go to the study, Anne is left by herself in the kitchen. Seeing Anne alone, Marthe sneaks into the house and begs to be hidden. She tells Anne that if she is caught they will burn her at the stake. Marthe commands Anne to help her because she helped Anne's mother when she was denounced as a witch. Anne denies her mother was a witch, but Marthe tells Anne that Absalon set her mother free so he could marry her. Upon hearing this story, Anne reluctantly agrees to let Marthe hide in her home.

5. Townspeople come to Absalon and Anne's home, claiming that little children saw Marthe enter their house. They search the home and capture her. Marthe pleads with Absalon for her life. Amidst Marthe's screams, Absalon bemoans the fact that the joyful day of his son's return is ruined.

6. Marthe is taken to the church and is interrogated. The clergy issues the following order:

> I order that the Notary of the Chapter, the Reverend Absalon Pedersson, take the said Heriot's Marthe to confession.

> He shall diligently exhort her to confess the full truth that she may not die without penance, but her soul be saved.

During the interrogation, Anne enters the church and overhears Marthe ask Absalon for help, the same help he afforded Anne's mother. She accuses him of knowing that Anne's mother was a witch and remaining silent. Absalon replies that Marthe should not beg for her life but instead pray for her soul.

7. During Marthe's interrogation, children are practicing the song they will sing when she is burned at the stake:

> Day of Wrath, Day of Mourning
> See fulfilled the prophet's warning.
> Oh, what fear man's soul renders
> When from Heaven
> The Judge descends.

8. Though Absalon has the power to save Marthe, he refuses. Marthe does not betray Absalon. He signs the final verdict, which reads:

> Heriot's Marthe was subjected to painful interrogation, after which she made a full voluntary confession in the presence of the assembled clergy.
> June 14, 1623
> Absalon Pedersson
> Jorgen Ravn

9. Time passes and Martin and Anne are shown cavorting in the fields. They are carefree and falling in love. The mood is broken when they see a wagon full of branches going to town. Martin correctly surmises the wood will be used for Marthe's execution. Before her execution, Marthe angrily tells Absalon that he has failed her. She threatens Absalon by saying that if she burns at the stake, so shall Anne.

10. During the execution, Anne leaves the site and goes into a building to watch from a window. Martin also leaves, declaring, "I can't stand this." Schoolchildren are brought to watch and sing.

11. After the execution, Absalon writes a report of the execution of Marthe, saying, "On the beauteous day, Heriot's Marthe was successfully

burned at the stake. Glory be to God." Marthe's execution haunts Absalon. He has serious doubts and prays aloud to God. His mother, Meret, overhears him and tells him he can tell her anything, but Absalon says he needs to think through things by himself. Absalon's mother tells him that she sees how Anne's eyes burn, just like her mother's eyes burned, and that Anne's mother confessed she had the power of invocation to call up the living and the dead. Absalon's mother says that someday, he will have to make a choice between Anne and God.

12. Anne asks Absalon if he spared her mother to marry her. Anne wonders at the power of her mother to bring forth the living and the dead with the help of the "Evil One." She likes the idea of having supernatural powers and tests her ability by calling Martin's name several times. He appears, thus proving to her that she is a witch. Both Absalon and Martin focus on Anne's eyes, each with a different perspective. Absalon states that her eyes are pure and childlike, while Martin sees them as mysterious.

13. Anne and Martin go to a stand of birch trees and profess their love for each other, while a tormented Absalon ponders his relationship with God. Later, after dinner, Anne is obviously happy and full of laughter. Absalon notes that this is the first time he has ever heard her laugh. He, along with Martin and his mother, notes how Anne has changed suddenly. She has become carefree and oblivious to the concerns of those around her. Alone with Martin, Anne tries to get him to commit to her.

14. Absalon leaves to help a critically ill man meet his death. The man had been cursed by Marthe during the time he was interrogating her. She told him that if she dies, he will soon follow. During Absalon's absence, Martin and Anne are together. Anne has dreams of sharing her life with Martin. She tells him that she wishes Absalon dead so they can be together. During this same time, Absalon's mother tells Martin that she hates Anne and suspects her of being a witch.

15. After the man's death, Absalon returns home during a terrible storm. His mother greets him and wants to talk, but Absalon wants to be alone. He says he is tired, but he can't rest and he feels that death is approaching him. He sees Anne and asks if she ever wished him dead. He believes he has been unfair to her, saying he took her joy and her youth. Anne angrily

retorts that she has wished him dead a hundred times. He brought her no joy, and he couldn't even give her a child. She admits her involvement with Martin. Brokenhearted and suspecting she is a witch, Absalon asks if she has the power of death over him. He leaves the room while calling his son's name and dies.

16. At the inquest into the circumstances of Absalon's death, Anne asks Martin whether he will support her if Meret, her mother-in-law, accuses her of being a witch. Martin sorrowfully says that he wishes he were dead, claiming everything is over now. Martin asks Anne if she caused her father's death, and she denies it. Martin believes her.

17. At the funeral, Absalon's mother says that if Martin won't tell the truth about Anne, she will. She announces that her son was murdered by Anne and denounces Anne as a witch. Martin, at this point, believes his grandmother. Anne is asked to lay her hand on the dead and take an oath that she is not a witch. Martin opens the coffin and has Anne sit next to Absalon. She finally admits that she killed him with the help of the Evil One and that she lured Martin into her power. The final words of the film are "Now you know."

Vocabulary

A lengthy list of words and phrases from the subtitles of this film is provided. From this list teachers can choose the words most appropriate for their classes. Words appear in chronological order so they may be introduced and reviewed as needed.

denounced
gnawing doubt
citizens
terrible darkness
herbs
tormenting
gallows
arrested
power in evil
strange
scandalous
power of invocation
cupboard
quivering flame
rectory
wretched woman
bloodstains
sermon

confession
atone
release her
eternity
consented
bog
evil
innocent
Devil
vigil
sacrament
interceding
beseech
coffin
courage
tormented
painful interrogation
expired
prattle
unavenged
condemned

Before the Movie

1. Why do you think people were persecuted as witches? What did people fear?

2. Do you think there were or are witches? If your answer is "yes," do you think witchcraft should be stopped?

During the Movie

1. Reflect on the song the children are singing in preparation for Marthe's execution. See number 7 in the outline of events on page 106 for the words to the song. Do you think the children knew what they were singing? How did the culture of the times contribute to the children's attitudes toward execution?

2. What are some examples of possible supernatural acts in the story?

After the Movie

1. What evidence was shown that indicated Anne was a witch?

2. If Anne's mother was a witch, would Anne be a witch too?

3. What do you think will happen to Anne?

Language Arts Activities

1. Young boys from the village sang "Day of Wrath, Day of Mourning" during Marthe's execution. The song continued with these words:

> Heaven and earth
> In ashes burning;
> Oh, what fear man's soul renders
> When from Heaven,
> The Judge descends,
> On whose sentence all depends.
> Wondrous sounds
> The trumpet sings.

Write a question concerning the meaning of the song. Discuss the questions as a whole group or in small groups. Before the discussion, model how to use prior knowledge, values, and feelings to make sense of the words. (language arts standard 3)

2. List and discuss incidences of cause and effect from the story. Determine whether you think the effect is caused by natural or supernatural forces. (language arts standards 2 and 3)

3. Candlelit rooms, shadows, and a violent storm set the mood for the story. Write a brief story using imagery to convey the mood and message of your story. (language arts standards 5 and 6)

Social Studies Activities

1. Research witchcraft and witch hunts in Europe. What events in Europe during the 1500s and 1600s might have precipitated the belief that witches were responsible for the evils of the world? What subsequent events in the later 1600s lessened the interest in pursuing people considered to be witches? (social studies standards I, II, and IV)

2. Absalon signed the final verdict. See number 8 in the outline of events on page 106 for a copy of the verdict. Marthe did not have any of the due process rights guaranteed to American citizens. Trace the history of our judicial system, from the Magna Carta (1215) to the habeas corpus

of 1679 to present-day U.S. law. Determine whether Danish law is based on the same documents as U.S. law. How does the U.S. system of justice compare with the system experienced by Marthe? Describe the rights that would be afforded to Marthe if she were tried for witchcraft today. (social studies standard VI)

Related Resources

Fiction

Gallows Hill by Lois Duncan
Thinner by Stephen King
Beyond the Burning Time by Kathryn Lasky
The Crucible: A Play in Four Acts by Arthur Miller
In the Devil's Snare: The Salem Witchcraft Crisis of 1692 by Mary Beth Norton
Witch Child by Celia Rees
A Break With Charity: A Story About the Salem Witch Trials by Ann Rinaldi
The Witches of Worm by Zilpha Keatley Snyder
Witch of Blackbird Pond by Elizabeth George Speare

Websites

Fordham University web page (www.fordham.edu/halsall/source/witches1.html)
Internet Medieval Source Book (www.fordham.edu/halsall/sbook.html), edited by Paul Halsall, which contains the following articles:

"The Ant Hill," Johannes Nider, 1437
"Summis desiderantes," Pope Innocent VIII, December 5, 1484
"The Hammer of Witches," Johannes Nider, 1486

EAST/WEST

Grade Level: 9–12
Filmed: 1999 in color
Genre: Historical drama
Time: 121 minutes
Language: French and Russian
Director: Regis Wargnier

Rating: PG-13 (some violence and a brief adult situation)
Theme: Josef Stalin's Soviet Russia, even when it didn't kill its own adherents, destroyed them.
Interesting Fact: The story is based on actual events as told by a number of survivors.
Setting: Post-World War II Soviet Union from 1946 to 1958. Odessa, a seaport on the Black Sea, and Kiev.

Summary

During the turmoil of the Bolshevik Revolution in 1917, millions of Russians fled their homeland; many emigrated from Russia to France. In the wake of World War II, many accepted Stalin's invitation to return to Russia and his guarantee of amnesty. Thousands of expatriates joyfully anticipated the return to their motherland, only to learn upon arrival that they had been led into a trap. Dominated by a fanaticism to keep Russian citizens from knowing about freedom and the higher standard of living in the West, Stalin ordered the murder of ex-POWs and thousands of innocent civilians who arrived in Russia to participate in the rebuilding after the devastation caused by World War II. A few people who could provide needed services are spared and forced to live in crowded substandard conditions, always fearing for their lives.

This film follows the plight of one expatriate family—a doctor, Alexei, his wife, Marie, and his young son, Sergei. After a brutal interrogation, the family is allowed to stay in Russia because Alexei's skills as a doctor are needed. They have been living a comfortable life in France, but he, like many other patriots, answers the call for help from his motherland, a decision he and his family will deeply regret. Entering Russia with high expectations, Alexei and his wife quickly learn they are trapped in a cruel, vengeful country with little hope of escape. What makes the family's situation even more intolerable is that they voluntarily left their good life in France. Being the head of the family, Alexei is racked with guilt over his decision to return to Russia.

Scenes of the family coping with crowded and substandard living conditions provide vivid comparisons between life in communist Russia and the West. The relationship between Alexei and Marie becomes strained to the breaking point. Marie, desperate to escape with their young son, becomes involved with a swimmer who shares her goals. Daily they meet, and a romantic relationship develops. She helps him plot his escape, while he swims in icy waters to condition himself for the long swim to freedom. Meanwhile, Alexei is also working to plan an escape for his family. He learns he can only secure freedom for Marie and their young son. He must stay behind because he is a Soviet citizen and Party member.

Characters

Marie: French wife of Alexei and lover of Sacha. She accompanies her husband to Russia when he accepts Stalin's offer of repatriation.

Alexei: Husband of Marie and a physician who answers Stalin's invitation to be repatriated. Realizing he has put his family at risk, he works to help them escape.

Sergei: The young son of Marie and Alexei who came to Russia with his parents as a young boy and grows into a young man.

Alexander (Sacha): Young Soviet swimmer, plotting to defect after his grandmother was forcibly taken from her home and killed because she spoke and sang in French.

Gabrielle: Famous French actress and political activist. She helps Marie and Sergei escape from Russia.

Colonel Boyko: Director of the Red Army Chorus. Unwittingly enables Marie to help Sacha escape Russia.

Outline of Events

Prologue:

June 1946, a dispatch

The news is out among the embassies of France, Bulgaria, and Yugoslavia. To all the former citizens of the Russian Empire who left during the Revolution of 1917 who wanted a passport. A passport will be issued to them which attests to their Soviet nationality. The new citizens can ask that they be repatriated in the Soviet Union.

There were thousands who came back to enter their homeland. These people were the last travelers of the dark years which had displaced throughout Europe more than 30 million men, women, and children over the last five years.

1. Joyful and hopeful, Russian expatriates return home to Russia to help in the rebuilding after World War II. Instead they find that they have been tricked into returning so they could be killed or imprisoned. It is Stalin's revenge and guarantee that they will not spread stories of affluence about the West.

2. Alexei, Marie, and their young son, Sergei, part of a group of expatriates, are spared and allowed to become assimilated into Russian life because of the need for doctors. However, conditions are drastically different from the comfortable life they left behind in France. They are forced to live in a small apartment shared by five other families. People are hostile and suspicious.

3. Marie can't take the pressure of the danger posed by the secret police after witnessing the arrest of one of the few women who had been friendly to her. She had been caught singing French songs, a crime that cost Marie's friend her life.

4. Marie misses her family and her style of living and desperately wants to return to France. At this time she is naïve, thinking her family can leave Russia and return to France. She begs her husband to help them leave, but the situation seems hopeless.

5. Marie meets a famous actress, Gabrielle, and pleads with her to deliver a letter to the French Embassy to rescue her family.

6. Knowing she is trapped in the Soviet Union, Marie plots to find a way out. She accompanies a young swimmer, Sacha, when he goes to Odessa, a seaport on the Black Sea, to train as a swimmer. They scheme to find passage out of Russia on a ship from Odessa. During the time Sacha is training for his marathon swim to freedom, they become romantically involved.

7. Sacha makes his daring escape. He swims for several hours in the Black Sea to meet a Turkish ship at the rendezvous point. He dodges detection by a Russian ship and is finally picked up by the Turkish captain. Marie is unable to escape because of the scrutiny of the KGB. Her husband,

Alexei, finds out about his wife's infidelity and her plans to leave Russia. He assures her that he is doing all he can to help her and their son escape.

8. Marie is accused by the secret police of helping Sacha escape and is sent to a work camp to serve a 10-year sentence. She is released after 6 years because of the efforts of her husband Alexei.

9. Alexei secretly makes arrangements with Gabrielle, the French actress, to secure passports for Marie and their son. He helps them escape to the French Embassy in Bulgaria. Alexei is left behind to deal with a highly suspicious secret police, who punish him for not informing them of his wife's plan to escape.

10. Sacha finds a new life in Canada, and Marie and Sergei safely return to France. Alexei is sent as a medic to a labor camp on the far east island of Sakhalin. He is permitted to return to France, 40 years after he left, in 1987 during the Gorbachev perestroika era.

Vocabulary

A lengthy list of words and phrases from the subtitles of this film is provided. From this list teachers can choose the words most appropriate for their classes. Words appear in chronological order so they may be introduced and reviewed as needed.

displaced
informing
motherland
supervisor
country
funeral
rebuilding
modern convenience
fascism
babushka (grandmother)
Soviet government
executed
prison

imperialist spy
exploits
colonial
communist
passengers
secret service
foreigner
Queen of England
champion
emigrants
celebrate
laundry
passports

tenants
deported
translate
Orthodox Church
arrested
hesitation
citizen
volunteers
performance
compatriots
Communist Party
Comrade Stalin
diplomat
Interior Ministry
embassy
factory
Turkish captain

Before the Movie

1. Recall a time when you were tricked by a false promise. How did you react? What were the consequences?

2. Read about Stalin. What were his goals?

During the Movie

1. Why can't Alexei, Marie, and their young son leave Russia?

2. How have their freedoms been limited?

3. Compare the crowded living conditions in Russia in the 1940s with living conditions today.

After the Movie

1. What events caused a strain on the relationship between Marie and Alexei?

2. Put yourself in Alexei's place. Why would a physician with a family emigrate from France to Russia in 1946 when he had to know the nature of Stalin's government?

Language Arts Activities

1. Marie was extremely unhappy with her new life in Russia. Assuming the role of Marie, write a letter home to France describing your life in Russia. (language arts standard 5)

2. Little was seen of Alexei and Marie's young son. Create a schedule you think would represent the events in a typical day for a young child in 1946 Russia. (language arts standard 5)

3. Write a journal from the perspective of Alexei, beginning with his life in France. (language arts standard 5)

4. Create a timeline of events from the time Russian expatriates received Stalin's invitation to return to Russia to the time Alexei was allowed to leave Russia. Choose one of the events and change it. Rewrite the timeline to reflect a different course of events because of the change of a single event. (language arts standards 5, 6, and 7)

5. Imagine you are a reporter for the American press. Write a newspaper account of the expatriates arriving in Russia. Write follow-up stories on the secret police, living conditions, athletics, and defections. (language arts standards 5, 6, and 7)

6. To understand how Stalin's utter disregard for the value of life has personal and global implications, read about the life of Zworykin, a man whose contribution directly affects our lives today. Vladimir Zworykin, the pioneer of television, was one of the Russians who fled his country to go to the United States after the Bolshevik Revolution. Think of him as you remember the deaths of people trying to reenter their beloved homeland to help in its reconstruction. How many contributions have been lost to the world because of Stalin? Write a story describing what might have happened if Zworykin, an eminent physicist and inventor, had answered Stalin's call to return to Russia immediately after World War II. Would the Russians have used him as a propaganda victory versus the West, or would Stalin have killed him as punishment for leaving the Soviet Union in 1917? (language arts standards 1, 2, 5, 7, and 8)

Social Studies Activities

1. To provide a background leading up to the plight of Alexei and his family, outline major events in Russian history from the Bolshevik Revolution, when people first fled Russia, to perestroika (i.e., from 1917 to 1987). Connect the history of Russia during this time to events in the film. (social studies standards V and VI)

2. What were the differences between the tsarist regimes and communist dictatorship? (social studies standard VI)

3. Read about Stalin. Describe Stalin's motivations to extend a welcome home to the expatriates, when his intent was to kill or imprison them. (social studies standard VI)

4. Create a map of the route the ship carrying French émigrés must have taken to travel from Marseille, France, to the Odessa seaport. Show the circuitous route the ship had to travel. Make a list of the countries adjacent to the waterways the ship passed through. List the names of the seas. Measure the distances between landforms, and determine the narrowest and widest spans of water. (social studies standard III)

5. Alexei and his family were assigned a communal apartment by the Russian government. State allocation of living space is much different from how most people live in the West. Compare postwar living conditions between Russia and another country in the West. (social studies standards I and V)

6. Sacha arranged for a Turkish sea captain to pick him up at sea. Locate Odessa on a map. How far is Odessa from Bulgaria? Find the closest route to freedom. If Sacha swam for six hours, how far do you think he would have traveled from Odessa? How far do you think he would have to swim to avoid detection by the Russians? (social studies standard III)

7. The Russian government punished citizens who tried to defect from the Soviet Union. In the film the swimmer and the coach were warned that they would pay if Sacha defected. What do you think happened to the coach after the defection of the swimmer? (social studies standard I)

8. The Soviets held a very different view of athletics than did Western nations. They viewed every interaction with other countries as a means of advancing and glorifying communism. Athletic events were state sponsored, with the government taking an active interest in the performance of its athletes. Read about athletic competitions during Soviet times, and compare the Soviet Union's treatment of its athletes with the treatment of athletes in the West. How were Russian athletes treated when they returned to the Soviet Union after losing a competition? (social studies standards VI and X)

Related Resources

Fiction

Angel on the Square by Gloria Whelan

Nonfiction

Zworykin, Pioneer of Television by Albert Abramson
Black Sea by Neal Ascherson
Stalin: Breaker of Nations by Robert Conquest
The Black Sea: A History by Charles King
Stalin: The First In-Depth Biography Based on Explosive New Documents From Russia's Secret Archives by Edvard Radzinsky

GRAND ILLUSION

Grade Level: 9–12
Time: 111 minutes
Filmed: 1938 in black and white
Language: French and German
Genre: Historical
Director: Jean Renoir
Rating: Not rated
Theme: The sense of honor and duty overcomes the solidarity of class.
Interesting Fact: This is often cited as one of the greatest war films ever made and, furthermore, one of the greatest films ever made. It was meant to show the futility of war, but it is ironic that it was made in 1937, just two years before the start of the World War II, the most destructive war in history.
Setting: German prisoner of war camps in 1916 during World War I and a rural farm near the Swiss border.

Summary

Grand Illusion deals with the fact of human nature that enables French officers to fight and kill Germans in war yet receive polite and respectful treatment by the Germans in a French officer prison camp. Not only is there a gentility between each group, but as the officers get to know each other they find they have much in common. Mortal enemies on the battlefield become wary friends in the much smaller universe of a prison camp. Although on different sides of the "imaginary line," French Captain de Boeldieu and his counterpart on the German side, Commandant von Rauffenstein, find they have much in common with each other. Is war an illusion of differences and hatred?

Another theme explored in this film is man's sense of duty. Though German guards make life in the prison camp for French officers bearable and, at times, even pleasant, the French officers scheme and plot for ways to make their escape from the camp. German and French officers with debilitating war injuries long to return to the battlefield where, under the conditions of war, they would kill each other without regret. This film deals with paradoxes of human nature.

Most of the story takes place inside German POW camps and is seen through the perspectives of the German prison guards and French prisoners of war. Within the camps, the men's social class transcends nationalism and patriotism. The film ends with the death of a nobleman and the beginning of a future filled with possibilities for the members of the bourgeois and working class.

Characters

Commandant von Rauffenstein: German officer sidelined to run POW camps after battle injuries. He feels a kinship with others who share his nobility status.

Captain de Boeldieu: French aristocrat and career officer in the French Army.

Lieutenant Maréchal: Wounded during the downing of his plane. He is a member of the blue-collar class. He prefers cycling in the Tour de France to more elegant pastimes enjoyed by the nobility.

Captain Rosenthal: Comes from a wealthy Jewish family involved in banking. He receives generous packages of food and liquor, which he shares with the other prisoners.

The engineer: French officer who calculates all aspects of digging the escape tunnel, including its length, time of completion, and the disposal of large quantities of dirt.

Elsa: German widow who finds Maréchal and de Boeldieu hiding in her barn during their escape to Switzerland. She falls in love with Maréchal.

Lotte: Little girl who delights in the kind and lavish attention of Maréchal and Rosenthal.

Outline of Events

Prologue:

> This story happened in 1916 during the first world war, before the Americans came to help the European democracies in their fight for liberty.

1. The opening prologue foreshadows the real theme of this film: Europe's internecine battle for supremacy, resulting in the extinction of boundaries among social classes. This film, based on a story of French prisoners in German war camps, focuses not on the war but on man's connection to man based on his social class. World War I was the watershed among kings, dukes, and royalty. These noble positions were replaced by the democratic impulses that arose in the West and the militant and expansionist zealotry of communism and fascism that arose in central and eastern Europe.

2. When von Rauffenstein, a German officer and aviator, is told he shot down two French officers, Captain de Boeldieu and Lieutenant Maréchal, he orders that they be brought in for lunch. When not fighting on the battlefield, the German and French officers have a mutual respect for one another. The two French aviators are treated with all the respect of their rank but are, nevertheless, taken to a prisoner-of-war camp.

3. French prisoners are allowed to receive packages from home containing food and liquor. Captain Rosenthal, a French officer from a wealthy Jewish family, shares the contents of his package with the other prisoners. He marvels that a can of peas easily arrives from Paris, whereas the French prisoners are separated from their homeland by an uncrossable line of fire. The Germans are all too happy to let the French keep their food so they won't have to feed them.

4. The French officers are treated well and offered some luxuries. However, no amount of food or solicitous friendship can subdue their sense of duty; their reasons vary according to their social class. The working-class Maréchal says, "I just want to do like the rest." The middle-class engineer

notes, “It’s a spirit of contradiction; since I can’t fight, I’ve been dying to.” Rosenthal, a member of the bourgeois, states, “I want to escape to defend my wealth.” And de Boeldieu, the nobleman, is more resigned to his position, saying, “To me the question doesn’t arise. A golf course is to play on, a tennis court also. A prison camp’s to be escaped.”

5. Together the French officers, all for different reasons, work to escape. They plan their escape by digging a tunnel from their cell to the garden outside the prison. During this time they learn that a fellow prisoner has just been shot for trying to escape. Though sobered, they are not deterred from continuing with their own escape plans.

6. During mail call, the French prisoners are allowed to read German newspapers. The accounts of German victories reported in the papers are considered to be exaggerated by the French. They question why there have been no celebrations of victory, including the raisings of flags and ringing of bells.

7. The digging of the escape tunnel continues. One of the French prisoners is an engineer who is able to calculate the distance the tunnel must run. He plans for the prisoners to dispose of the dirt by hiding it in bags in their pants legs and emptying them in the prison garden.

8. The prisoners put on a musical; they dress as women to entertain each other and the Germans. Captain de Boeldieu observes the frivolity concurrent with the clumsy marching of a group of young German soldiers, saying, “On one side children are playing as soldiers [marching], on the other, soldiers playing as children [dressing up].”

9. Douaumont, a French city, is captured, much to the dismay of the French. The French know this is not an exaggerated story because this time the report is accompanied by the raising of flags and the ringing of bells. However, soon thereafter it is retaken by the French. Maréchal leads the French prisoners in a display of patriotism. They sing their national anthem in front of the Germans. For this, Maréchal is placed in solitary confinement.

10. The French officers have completed their tunnel. Maréchal returns and joins the others. But on the day of their planned escape, the French prisoners are abruptly moved to another camp. They try to tell newly cap-

tured English prisoners about the tunnel, but because of the language barrier, the English don't understand. The French officers can only hope the English prisoners will find and use the tunnel they built.

11. After being moved several times, de Boeldieu, Rosenthal, and Maréchal arrive at another prison and find their German acquaintance from the first POW camp, von Rauffenstein, as the commandant. The commandant bemoans the fact that officers are no longer exclusively from the noble class. He confides to de Boeldieu that he had been badly injured in battle and can no longer serve his country on the battlefield. He longs to be back in battle, not sidelined as the commandant of a prison.

12. Though treated humanely, Captain de Boeldieu, Rosenthal, and Maréchal plan again to escape. They will use a long rope to climb down the steep walls of the fortress.

13. A large box from the tsar of Russia arrives. Thinking it contains food and liquor, the Russian and French prisoners and the German guards hold high expectations. When they find the box contains books, they are disappointed, and the Russian prisoners light the entire package on fire. The fire is a major distraction to the German guards, giving de Boeldieu, Rosenthal, and Maréchal an idea for their escape; they must come up with a distraction.

14. De Boeldieu insists on being the diversion for the escape. He realizes that at the war's end, he will no longer have a place in society, whereas opportunities for Maréchal and Rosenthal will be opening; they, not he, represent the future.

15. At the time of the escape, the French officers create a commotion, first by playing flutes and then banging on pots. All prisoners are ordered to the yard for roll call. De Boeldieu does not join them; when his name is called, he is heard playing a flute inside the building. As planned, this creates the diversion that allows Maréchal and Rosenthal to escape. De Boeldieu leads the Germans on a chase before being shot by the commandant.

16. Mortally wounded, de Boeldieu is visited by an apologetic commandant in the hospital. Von Rauffenstein tells de Boeldieu that he was clumsy; he tried to shoot him in the leg, not the stomach, and asks for his

forgiveness. De Boeldieu tells the commandant that he would have done the same thing in his place. He confides that his is a useless existence. He tells von Rauffenstein, "For a man of the people, it's terrible to die in the war; for you and me, it's a good solution."

17. Maréchal and Rosenthal escape. They become cold and hungry during their trek to neutral Switzerland. Rosenthal injures his ankle, which greatly slows their progress. They briefly lose patience with one another, but soon support each other during their walk. They come upon a small farm and seek shelter in the barn. A widow, Elsa, finds them and invites them into the house, where she offers them food and tends to Rosenthal's ankle.

18. Time passes. The French officers befriend not only Elsa but also her little girl, Lotte. Widowed and lonely, Elsa falls in love with Maréchal. She says she loves hearing footsteps in her home once again. However, Maréchal and Rosenthal must leave and continue their escape to Switzerland. Maréchal promises to return after the war.

19. Maréchal and Rosenthal leave, saying, "We have to finish the war, and let's hope it's the last. . . . An illusion." Trying to avoid detection by the Germans, they seek the border that is "manmade and invisible." They are spotted by the Germans, who begin to shoot at them but stop when they realize their targets have crossed the invisible border into Switzerland.

Vocabulary

A lengthy list of words and phrases from the subtitles of this film is provided. From this list teachers can choose the words most appropriate for their classes. Words appear in chronological order so they may be introduced and reviewed as needed.

headquarters
coal shovel
Camembert
present
squadron
suffocation
alcohol kills

innocent face
division headquarters
signal
photograph
crawling
canal
phooey

resolve
naturalized French
preference
patriotism
congratulations
vegetarian
hospital
artistic performance
wounded
tulips
pilot
I don't understand French
military attaché
disguised
mechanic
amusing
coincidence
patriotic courage
prisoner-of-war camp
German barbarism
camp regulations
attention
strictly forbidden
bureaucrat
congregate
exaggerate
civilians strictly prohibited
embarrassed
formality
confiscate the flutes
jailors
civilian authorities
Tour de France
stomach
pickled mackerel
slipped
generosity
hungry

Before the Movie

1. In your experience, how do people express their patriotism?

2. What do you consider your most important duty? Would you be willing to give your time, devote extra work, or risk your life to fulfill your duty?

3. This film is known as an antiwar film. Look for evidence of antiwar sentiment as you view the film.

During the Movie

1. Compare and contrast the behavior of men during battle and their behavior at the prison camp. What causes men to act differently toward each other in different situations?

2. How did the French express their patriotism while in prison?

After the Movie

1. It was implied that Elsa lost not only her husband in the war but also other male members of her family. Why would she freely offer assistance to men who fought for the enemy? What would you have done if you were in her place?

2. Do you think Maréchal will return to France and reunite with Elsa and Lotte?

3. How do you think it is possible for men to seek to kill each other on the battlefield and enjoy each other's company when they are away from battle? When, if ever, do you think social class plays a role in men's feelings about each other?

4. Ironically, this antiwar movie was filmed in 1938, one year before the beginning of World War II. Do you think the director Renoir's views changed when faced with the menace of Hitler?

Language Arts Activities

1. The French prisoners did not believe the newspaper accounts of German victories. Choose a current events topic. Read about your topic from several different sources. Do you perceive a bias? How do the accounts vary? (language arts standard 1)

2. Compare the attitudes of four of the main characters on serving their country.

Maréchal (working class): "I just want to do like the rest."

The engineer (middle class): "It's a spirit of contradiction; since I can't fight, I've been dying to."

Rosenthal (bourgeois class): "I want to escape to defend my wealth."

de Boeldieu (nobility class): "To me the question doesn't arise. A golf course is to play on, a tennis court also. A prison camp's to be escaped."

(language arts standard 3)

3. Research the countries involved in World War I. Make a chart of the primary participants, labeling one side of the chart "Allies" and the other side "Central Powers." Locate each of the countries on a map and mark them

as either Allies or Central Powers. In small groups, first choose a country from the central powers. Write an apologetic stating why that country is involved in the war. Repeat for the allied countries. (language arts standard 7)

4. Using the World War II game *Axis and Allies* by Milton Bradley as a prototype, develop a World War I game, *Central Powers and Allies*. (language arts standard 7)

5. The use of airplanes in war began during World War I. Though primitive by today's standards, many aviators became famous for their daring and heroics during World War I. German aviator Baron Manfred von Richthofen and American aviator Eddie Rickenbacker have become legends. Use music, art, oratory, or writing to communicate the feats of each of these fliers. Play the popular 1960s song *The Red Baron*, by the Royal Guardsmen, to introduce this activity. (language arts standards 1, 4, 7, and 8)

Social Studies Activities

1. Maréchal and de Boeldieu were flying a reconnaissance plane over Germany when they were shot down. The first military planes were crudely constructed and used primarily for reconnaissance. Make an illustrated chart of the history of aircraft used in war. (social studies standards II and VIII)

2. Both Maréchal and Rosenthal had plans to return to the war and fight for France after their escape from the prisoner-of-war camp. Read about France's involvement in World War I. Where would they most likely have been sent? (social studies standard II)

3. Boundaries between countries played a significant role in the film. Prisoners marveled at the fact that a can of peas could easily cross boundaries that they could not. Boundaries between countries were described as "invisible boundaries" not created by nature. Look at a map of the countries involved in World War I. Determine which boundaries are defined by natural landforms and water and which ones are not discernible ("invisible"). Explain how you think the boundaries between two countries were created. (social studies standard III)

4. Make a map and timeline of events that took place between the 1914 assassination of Austria–Hungary's Archduke Francis Ferdinand and the 1916 portrayal of French officers held in a German prison. (social studies standards II and III)

Related Resources

Fiction

All Quiet on the Western Front by Erich Maria Remarque

Nonfiction

Biography of the Late Marshal Foch by George Aston
French Aircraft of the First World War by James Davilla and Arthur Soltan
The Red Baron's Last Flight: A Mystery Investigated by Norman Franks and Alan Bennett
Over Here: The First World War and American Society by David M. Kennedy
The First Air War: 1914–1918 by Lee Kennett
Talking With the Red Baron: Interviews With Manfred Von Richthofen by Peter Kilduff and Manfred Richthofen
The Guns of August by Barbara Tuchman
The Proud Tower by Barbara Tuchman
Black Jack: The Life and Times of John J. Pershing by Frank Everson Vandiver

THE HIDDEN FORTRESS

Grade Level: 9–12
Filmed: 1958 in black and white
Genre: Action, comedy
Rating: Not rated
Time: 139 minutes
Language: Japanese
Director: Akira Kurosawa
Theme: Greed undermines friendship and the ultimate good of the people.

Interesting Fact: *Star Wars* was inspired by this film. If *The Hidden Fortress* inspired George Lucas to create the epic *Star Wars*, it might just inspire reluctant readers to find pleasure in reading.
Setting: In the rocky mountainous country of 16th-century Japan.

Summary

A comedic adventure that takes place in the aftermath of a civil war fought between the territories of Akizuki and Yamana. Matashichi and Tahei, two bumbling Akizuki soldiers, having fought on the losing side, are trying to escape from Akizuki to get to the neutral territory of Hayakawa. They have just escaped from a prison where they spent their days burying the dead. They are constantly bickering along the way. In spite of insults hurled at each other, they remain together, frequently reaffirming their friendship. They are planning their escape to Hayakawa by going through the enemy territory of Yamana to avoid the heavily guarded border between Akizuki and Hayakawa.

The inept actions and greedy dispositions of Matashichi and Tahei hinder their escape. They meet up with a stranger, Rokurota, when he comes upon their campsite. He is a strong, mysterious man of few words. Though fearful he will find two sticks of gold they just found, Matashichi and Tahei become intrigued when he hints of having a large stash of gold. Eager to be accepted by the mysterious man so they can find his gold, Matashichi and Tahei show him their plan for escaping into the Hayakawa territory. Rokurota is impressed and lets them join forces with him. Rokurota wants to smuggle the Akizuki gold from the occupied territory to Hayakawa to use for the restoration of the Akizuki clan. He also has assumed responsibility for helping Princess Yuki Akizuki escape from the Akizuki territory and reclaim her throne.

Unknown to Matashichi and Tahei, the mysterious man is an Akizuki general. Along the way, General Rokurota encounters the enemy and competes in a lengthy duel with their leader, Hyoei Tadokoro; Rokurota wins but spares the life of his opponent. The outcome of the duel has a significant impact on the lives of the princess, the general, Matashichi, Tahei, and a slave girl they rescued along the way.

Facing the enemy every step of the way, eventually everyone makes it across the border into Hayakawa. Matashichi and Tahei are rewarded for their endurance with a single gold bar, which they must share. With an exaggerated show of generosity they begin to argue, each wanting the other to have the gold. They pledge to be kind to each other and go home as friends. Rokurota and Princess Yuki vow to use the rest of the gold to restore their homeland of Akizuki.

Characters

Matashichi and Tahei: Farmers who sold their homes for arms so they could seek their fortunes in the war. They escaped after fighting in Japan's civil war on the side of the Akizukis.

General Rokurota Makabe: A John Wayne–style hero. He easily becomes the leader of two ragtag men trying to escape enemy territory. He successfully restores Princess Yuki to the Akizuki throne and brings back their gold.

Princess Yuki Akizuki: Young and beautiful, she is the deposed Akizuki princess.

Slave girl: Young slave girl seen by Princess Yuki being physically and verbally abused. She is bought by General Rokurota and refuses to leave his side.

Hyoei Tadokoro: Disgraced enemy leader who loses a duel to General Rokurota. He ultimately defects and joins General Rokurota and the princess in their escape to the Hayakawa territory.

Outline of Events

1. Matashichi and Tahei, having just escaped from a prison in the Akizuki territory, are walking through the dusty, rocky Japanese countryside trying to get to the neutral territory of Hayakawa. They had fought for the Akizukis and lost to the Yamanas in a civil war. Neither is a leader; both bicker and insult each other as they struggle to find their way to the Hayakawa territory.

2. As Matashichi and Tahei travel toward the neutral territory of Hayakawa, they see the spearing of another Akizuki warrior trying to es-

cape. Tahei wants to strip the dead man of his possessions; Matashichi is opposed. They argue and part ways. Matashichi goes into town, where he sees a poster offering a reward for the capture of Princess Yuki Akizuki. A reward of 10 ryos is offered to anyone who finds her, and 3 ryos is offered to an informer. During the brief time Matashichi is in town, enemy soldiers raid the town. He is rounded up with hundreds of other people and sent to prison. Meanwhile, Tahei remains in the countryside, looking for a way to cross the border. Seeing that the border is heavily guarded and hearing from others that "not even a mouse can pass," Tahei decides to wait for the protective cover of fog before attempting his escape. However, once the fog rolls in he can't see and becomes confused. Once again he is caught by the enemy and sent to prison.

3. Matashichi and Tahei meet again in prison, where they are forced to dig for the Akizuki gold. The enemy guards tell them they are now moles, not men. They are not allowed to stop digging until they find the missing gold. Working until exhaustion, the prisoners find no gold. An uprising occurs in the prison, and hundreds of men rush to escape. During a hail of gunfire and stampeding men, Matashichi and Tahei consider their situation hopeless. Clinging to each other, they await the inevitable, saying, "This is the end. Let's die together." When it becomes quiet, they look up and find they are alone; not one live person is left. They steal rice, and run away.

4. While trying to cook rice at their campsite, Matashichi and Tahei become irritated that the wood won't burn properly. Frustrated, they toss it aside and hear a metallic sound as it lands. They retrieve the stick and find gold, emblazoned with the Akizuki crest, hidden within the wood. Realizing the gold is hidden in wood, not in the prison where the prisoners were forced to dig, Matashichi and Tahei begin a frenetic search of all the wood in the area.

5. Matashichi and Tahei later notice their camp is being watched by a mysterious stranger. They hope to keep the gold a secret and wish he would go away. Unknown to Matashichi and Tahei, the stranger is an Akizuki general, General Rokurota Makabe. That night, the mysterious man disappears, and Matashichi and Tahei are relieved he is gone. However, he returns later and sits silently by their fire. Puzzled, they watch and try to

make small talk. Matashichi and Tahei draw a map in the dust of the Hayakawa, Akizuki, and Yamana territories to show the stranger how they intend to escape to Hayakawa. They plan to cross over the border from Akizuki into Yamana on their way to Hayakawa, explaining that the enemy will not be expecting soldiers from Akizuki to cross through enemy territory. Rokurota is impressed with their plan and joins forces with them.

6. Rokurota hints of having more gold but tells Matashichi and Tahei the gold is useless unless they get three men and three horses to carry it. Again, Rokurota suddenly leaves. Matashichi and Tahei follow him, and after a long struggle to climb the side of a rocky mountain, find Lord Akizuki's hidden fortress and Rokurota. He introduces himself as Rokurota Makabe, the Akizuki General. The men don't believe him, saying, "You don't fool us." Unknown to the men, Princess Yuki is hiding from the enemy at her family's fortress.

7. To fool everyone into thinking the princess is dead, Rokurota says he has turned her in for the reward. He shows Matashichi and Tahei bars of gold, claiming he received the reward for turning in the princess. The next day Matashichi and Tahei are told that the princess has been executed.

8. Rokurota tells the princess he fabricated a story about turning her in and her execution to stop others from hunting for her. She becomes upset when she learns that his 16-year-old sister, Kofuyu, died in her place, saying, "I hate it." Rokurota tells the princess that people must think she is dead because a disguise won't hide the fact she is nobility. To avoid detection, he tells her she will be passed off as a mute so her cultured voice will not give her away.

9. Rokurota steals three horses to carry the gold to Akizuki. He leads Matashichi and Tahei to the wood that contains the gold, which has been hidden in the spring water. They begin to retrieve the gold from the spring and bundle it to look like firewood. The gold is loaded on three horses and carried by three men, Rokurota, Matashichi, and Tahei, as they begin their escape out of Akizuki and into Hayakawa.

10. During their walk toward the border, Rokurota leaves the princess, Matashichi, and Tahei behind with the horses. Matashichi and Tahei, thinking the princess is a mute and can't hear them, plan openly to steal

the horses. They engage in a humorous pantomime of leading horses to water to trick her into releasing the horses to them. With no intention of returning, they leave.

11. During Matashichi and Tahei's escape, they leave the horses unattended to test the depth of the water they must cross. They see enemy soldiers and run looking for their horses, hoping to escape. The horses are not where they left them; Princess Yuki had followed them and taken the horses back with her. Matashichi and Tahei frantically run back to the princess and Rokurota to warn the general of the advancing enemy soldiers. Angrily calling them traitors, he tells them to take their gold and go. Matashichi and Tahei leave but don't get far before they are fired on by enemy soldiers. They ride back and beg Rokurota to let them stay, promising to behave.

12. As they continue their journey to Hayakawa, Rokurota, the princess, Matashichi, and Tahei, with their precious gold-filled firewood, join throngs of others who are crossing a bridge and entering a village. The men, nervous about being seen by crowds of people, question Rokurota. He tells them that it is easier to hide a stone among stones and men among men.

13. While in the village, the princess, playing the role of a mute, comes upon slave traders abusing a young girl. When the men see the princess, they want to buy her until they learn she is mute. She returns and demands that Rokurota buy the young girl from the slave traders, saying she can't stand to see people suffering. She tells Rokurota that though she must be mute, she can't make her heart mute. Reluctantly, he buys the girl, hoping to set her free. Instead, the frightened and grateful girl will not leave his side.

14. Because Rokurota and the others aroused suspicion when they showed the town's magistrate a gold Akizuki crest that they claimed to have found on Mount Suribachi to during their escape through the Yamana Territory, the enemy has put out a notice to stop a group of three horses and one girl. However, Rokurota has sold one of his horses and acquired a girl. He is now traveling with two horses and two girls, thus temporarily avoiding recognition. The group is attacked by enemy soldiers on horseback. Rokurota stabs one of the men; the others flee. He

chases the men to the enemy's compound, where he recognizes their leader, Hyoei Tadokoro. A lengthy duel with lances ensues. In the end, Rokurota defeats Hyoei, who simply says, "I've lost." Out of sympathy, Rokurota lets him live.

15. While Rokurota is engaged in the duel, the slave girl sees dozens of carts filled with firewood traveling to the Fire Festival. The enemy is checking the wood for hidden gold but soon gives up, declaring there are too many to check. She proposes they join the procession. They make it unchallenged to the festival. During the celebration Rokurota orders that they burn their load, cart and all. After, they sing the following song:

> Set fire to men's lives
> With the beneficial flame.
> Insects throw their life into the bonfire flames.
> Ponder and you'll see
> The world is darkness and
> The floating world's a dream;
> So burn in wild abandon.

16. The next day Rokurota, Princess Yuki, the slave girl, Matashichi, and Tahei dig through the ashes, picking up gold. The gold is heavy, and the group cannot take it all. Being greedy, Matashichi and Tahei pick up more than they can comfortably carry. Even with the heavy weight of the gold, Matashichi and Tahei return to the ashes to look for more. Enemy soldiers find them. Rokurota fights off the enemy and captures two of the enemy soldiers. He tells them to carry the gold or die. They help carry the gold, but once again the group encounters the enemy. The two captives try to escape and are shot by their own people. Matashichi and Tahei leave, deciding to approach the enemy as informers in hopes of getting a reward. The enemy does not believe them, and they leave in disgrace, making their way finally into the Hayakawa territory.

17. With the Hayakawa border in sight, Rokurota, the princess, and the slave girl are captured by the Yamana soldiers. They are tied up in prison and are to be executed the following day. Hyoei, the man who lost the duel to Rokurota, enters their cell. His face is badly disfigured. Claiming his life has not been worth living since the duel, he asks

Rokurota why he left him to live in disgrace, a form of refined cruelty, rather than kill him.

18. Rokurota, the princess, and the slave girl are being led to their execution. At the last minute, Hyoei intervenes, and they escape. Hyoei, saying, "Forgive me for defecting," joins the freed group and crosses into Hayakawa territory with Rokurota and the princess.

19. Meanwhile, Matashichi and Tahei make it to safety, but without any of the gold. Bedraggled and discouraged, they are bemoaning the lost gold. During this time of self-pity, horses carrying the gold run up to them. With shrieks of happiness and disbelief, they begin to take the horses. Again, they are caught by soldiers and imprisoned. Thinking they are about to be executed, they once again seek solace from each other. They are brought instead to Princess Yuki and Rokurota, who thank them for all they have endured and give them one bar of gold to share. Matashichi and Tahei, with a renewed appreciation of life, try to overcome their greed, professing their friendship. Princess Yuki, with General Rokurota and Hyoei at her side, vows to use the gold to restore the Akizuki clan.

Vocabulary

A lengthy list of words and phrases from the subtitles of this film is provided. From this list teachers can choose the words most appropriate for their classes. Words appear in chronological order so they may be introduced and reviewed as needed.

essence of stench
executed
dung beetle
restrain yourself
fortune
loyal retainers
sniveling face
sympathy
gravedigger
victim
stink ball
outwit the enemy
barrier
disguise
reward
emerging
ryo (currency)
territory
capture
contrary

informers
opposite approach
thieves
backbone
defeated
inconvenient
empty stomach
traitors
sword
won't budge
woodcutter
greedy fellow
bargain
proxy
divide equally
customers
mountains
slave trader
my throat's dry
reckless
general
rare encounter
partners
battlefield
equal shares
weapons
bullying
lance
business
Fire Festival
filthy teeth
suspicious
madness
greedy fellow
no ordinary man
informer
bluffing
refined cruelty

Before the Movie

Note: Because of the unfamiliar spelling of Japanese names, it would be helpful to list and review the names before showing the film. To demystify the names, provide students with a list of characters and the names of the territories.

1. Did you ever have to share something you really valued with your best friend? How much were you willing to share with your friend? How did it make you feel?

2. Picture technology in 16th-century Japan. What forms of transportation do you think people used? What weapons did they use for war and defense?

During the Movie

1. Draw and label a map of the three regions involved in the civil war.

2. Compare life in 16th-century Japan with life as you know it.

After the Movie

1. Compare the actions of the comical pair of men, Matashichi and Tahei, with those of General Rokurota Makabe. Whose actions do you think are most believable?

2. How do you think Matashichi and Tahei will cope with one bar of gold between them? Do you think the gold will bring them together as friends or make them enemies?

Language Arts Activities

1. Though not explicitly shown in the film, write a story describing what you think happened to Hyoei after losing the duel to General Rokurota. Include implications about the code of honor that led him to say he would rather be dead than left alive after losing the duel. What did Hyoei mean by the term "refined cruelty"? (language arts standards 3 and 6)

2. The meaning of the words from the song sung at the Fire Festival most likely became obscured when it was translated from Japanese into English. Cultural differences may also obscure the meaning of the song. Rewrite the song so it will be more meaningful and suitable to people today. (language arts standards 3 and 9)

3. Maintaining one's honor appears to be of primary importance in Japan during the 16th century. Two men, Matashichi and Tahei, added elements of comic relief to the story because their blatant emotional outbursts were the antithesis of expected honorable actions. Compare their actions with General Rokurota's. How did these men differ? Describe how comedy was used to convey the personalities of Matashichi and Tahei. What effect did comedy have on the story? (language arts standards 3, 6, and 9)

4. Women were dishonored in 16th-century Japan. Many young women were sold by slave traders. Research the treatment of women and their roles in 16th-century Japan. Compare information with the lives of present-day women. Present the information orally. (language arts standards 4, 7, and 8)

5. General Rokurota told Lord Akizuki that he brought Matashichi and Tahei to the fortress because he was impressed with their plans to escape

to Hayakawa. Thinking they were not too bright, Rokurota observed, "Necessity makes even fools think." Describe what he meant by this statement. Give examples to support Rokurota's statement from the film and from your experiences. (language arts standards 3 and 6)

Social Studies Activities

1. General Rokurota told Matashichi and Tahei that the gold was worthless if they couldn't carry it out of enemy territory. What they really needed were more men and horses to help them carry the gold. Determine what makes commodities valuable. If you were in the middle of hostile territory trying to find your way home, what commodities would you seek? (social studies standard VII)

2. Matashichi and Tahei were friends who were imprisoned and nearly killed several times. Though they traded insults, they stayed together as friends. Discuss factors that may have contributed to their friendship. (social studies standard IV)

3. Imagine you are Princess Yuki, the leader of the Akizuki clan, displaced and devastated by war. You have brought back enough gold to rebuild the clan. Research technology available in 16th-century Japan, and devise a plan for rebuilding the infrastructure necessary to restore goods and services to the community. Determine the wants and needs of your people, including the need for defense. (social studies standards VI, VII, and VIII)

4. Research life in 16th-century Japan. Determine problems that led to civil wars. Determine some solutions to the problems that may have prevented war. Write the ways technology today might have impacted events in 16th-century Japan. (social studies standard VIII)

Related Resources

Fiction

Commodore Perry in the Land of the Shogun by Rhonda Blumberg
The King's Fifth by Scott O'Dell
Of Nightingales That Weep by Katherine Paterson and Haru Wells

JEAN DE FLORETTE

Grade Level: 6–12 **Time:** 83 minutes
Filmed: 1986 in color **Language:** French
Genre: Drama **Director:** Claude Berri
Rating: PG (occasional use of strong language)
Theme: Lesser evils provide the seeds for greater evils.
Interesting Fact: *Manon of the Spring* is the sequel to *Jean de Florette*. A guide for the sequel is not included because of brief nudity at the beginning of the film.
Setting: The beautiful French countryside of Provence around 1919 after World War I. Two neighboring farms, the Soubeyran Farm and the Florette Farm, are the primary focus of the movie.

Summary

This is a story about sin, greed, blind optimism, and their consequences. It offers a rich social commentary on the effects of evil.

The Soubeyran farm has fertile soil but no natural water source; the Florette farm has fertile soil and a bountiful water source. Water is the sought-after prize by farmers.

Ugolin, a slightly dimwitted soldier, returns home from the war with some carnation plants. After planting them on his farm and tenderly caring for them, he is rewarded with a garden patch of beautiful blooms. The beauty of his flowers and the money he receives for selling them inspire a vision: Ugolin wants to grow fields of beautiful carnations. The problem is that his farm does not have enough water to sustain his vision. However, his aging relative, Papet, knows that a rich water source exists on the neighboring farm.

Papet and Ugolin offer to buy the land from their neighbor, Marius Bouffigue; when he refuses, he is accidentally killed by Papet during a fight. Ugolin's and Papet's hopes of buying the land from Bouffigue's heir are dashed when they learn that the heir's son, a man with a hunched back, and his family are moving from the city to take over the farm.

The malicious scheming of Papet and Ugolin to run the new family off the land creates hardships and ultimate tragedy. The story is about a highly optimistic and dedicated farmer desperately trying to save his crops and livestock in the face of a drought. A secret, kept by the neighbors and townspeople, could have saved his farm.

Characters

César (Papet) Soubeyran: A prominent farmer and middle-aged member of an established influential family. He is the brains behind the scheme to buy the neighboring farm.

Ugolin Galinette: Nephew of Papet. He is in line to inherit his uncle's farm. He is a slightly dimwitted dreamer who, in spite of occasional pangs of conscience, carries out the schemes of his uncle Papet.

Marius Bouffigue: Neighbor to Papet. He is killed as a result of a scuffle with Papet.

Florette de Berengère: Never shown in the film, she is the heiress of Marius Bouffigue's estate. She leaves the farm to her son and his family.

Jean Cadoret: Son of Florette. He inherits the farm when his mother dies. He is a decent, hardworking family man who desperately tries to become a successful farmer. Optimistic and smart, he is ridiculed by his neighbors for being an outsider and having a hunched back.

Aimée Cadoret: Loving and supportive wife of Jean. She is a former opera singer who gave up her career to move to the farm.

Manon Cadoret: A young girl who becomes involved in her parents' dreams and heartbreak. She ultimately learns the secret that had been kept from her parents and vows revenge.

Amandine: Housekeeper for Papet who is a deaf mute.

Outline of Events

1. Ugolin returns home from the war carrying a precious package of carnation plants. He dreams of raising fields of carnations and becoming rich, but there is no natural water source on the farm to support his dream.

2. Knowing a natural spring is on the land of the adjacent farm, Ugolin and Papet visit the owner, Marius Bouffigue, and offer to buy his land. He refuses and is killed by Papet in a fight.

3. When Ugolin and Papet learn that the farm will not be offered for sale but will be run by the son of the heir, Ugolin and Papet scheme to make farming impossible for the new owner.

4. Together they plug up and conceal the spring, a vital water source, and vandalize the house. They hoped that one glimpse of a run-down, dilapidated farm with no water source would drive off the new owner, clearing the way to buy the land, now depreciated, for a fraction of what it was really worth.

5. The new owner, Jean Cadoret, overcome by the beauty of the countryside, has his own dream for establishing a prosperous farm. No hardship is too great; when obstacles present themselves, he enthusiastically seeks solutions. He is an optimist who will let nothing separate him from his dream. Rather than being driven off by setbacks, the new family, trusting in God and their own hard work, try valiantly to overcome the hardships facing them. The barrier that stands between fulfilling the visions of the families of both farms is water.

6. Ugolin and Papet are wolves in sheep's clothing, giving the illusion of helping the Cadoret family while concealing the lifesaving secret of a spring. Trying to discourage the family from staying, they offer no encouragement and offer assistance only when they know their help will not be sufficient to solve the problems facing the family. These men display an occasional flicker of conscience as they observe the terrible toll their schemes are taking on the family, but greed is overpowering.

7. Occasional scenes of the townspeople show the distrust and dislike they have for the newcomer, Jean Cadoret, and his family. They refer to him as "the hunchback." Jean Cadoret's disfigurement makes him an object of ridicule. Many of the townspeople know of the spring that exists on his land, but no one tells him. They mutter to each other that it is none of their business and refuse to become involved.

8. In the end, Jean Cadoret takes a drastic measure, sure that this time he will produce water for his farm. Instead, tragedy strikes when Jean Cadoret, who is half-crazed by overwork, worry, and red wine, uses dynamite to blast an area he is sure will yield water. As soon as the blast occurs, he runs to the hole and is fatally wounded by flying rocks and debris. At this point Jean Cadoret's widow, Aimée, has no choice but to sell the farm.

9. Under the continued guise of helpfulness, Ugolin and Papet, reminding Aimée that the farm lacks a viable water source, make what they say is a generous offer to purchase the farm. She accepts.

10. Shortly after they become owners of the Florette farm, the greedy neighbors quickly unplug the spring and gleefully celebrate their victory. They are completely unaware that Manon, the daughter, is watching them from behind a clump of trees. Full comprehension of the events that had befallen her family shine brightly in her eyes.

Vocabulary

A lengthy list of words and phrases from the subtitles of this film is provided. From this list teachers can choose the words most appropriate for their classes. Words appear in chronological order so they may be introduced and reviewed as needed.

Marseille
othentics (authentic)
bachelor
disaster
orchard
conscience
flowers
landscape
florist
rabbits
carnations
public health hazard
cistern
sporadic
reservoir
proliferation
natural water source
squab
thousand franc bills
plough
horizontal
necklace
corpse
scorching summer
buckshot
it's urgent
heiress
emeralds were fake
inheritance
divining rod
accident
dowser
hunchback
mortgage
surveyor's map
dynamite
cultivate
clowned around

Before the Movie

1. Discuss students' experiences with growing plants and raising animals.

2. Discuss farming and the importance of water. Have students list everything they use water for in one day.

3. Discuss needs and wants. What is the difference?

During the Movie

1. Compare the water supply available to Jean Cadoret with the water supply where you live.

2. How do you think the greed of Jean Cadoret's neighbors will affect the success of his farm?

3. Who do you think, if anyone, will come to the aid of Jean Cadoret?

4. Will Jean or his family find a way to get water?

5. Why don't Aimée and Manon like Ugolin?

6. Does Jean's disfigurement hinder him?

7. Jean is defined by his deformity in spite of all he accomplished. Do you think this attitude is prevalent today?

After the Movie

1. Who was responsible for Jean Cadoret's death?

2. What responsibility did Jean Cadoret have for his own death?

3. Why did the townspeople keep the secret to themselves?

4. Do you think Jean Cadoret was a wise man or a fool?

5. What is meant by the saying "It is easier to push someone downhill than uphill"?

6. What do you think will happen if Manon tells her mother about what she saw at the spring?

7. Describe how life would have been different if knowledge of the spring had been revealed to Jean Cadoret.

8. How do farmers get water for their crops and livestock today?

9. Discuss the saying "Water is liquid gold."

Language Arts Activities

1. "Ugly exterior hides the purest souls." Relate this saying to the characters in the movie. (language arts standard 2)

2. When César "Papet" Soubeyran and his nephew, Ugolin, began their scheme to get the farm, a domino effect occurred. Each evil act led to other unforeseen acts. Create a cause and effect timeline or a graphic organizer indicating the causal event and subsequent effects. (language arts standard 7)

3. Read books about farm families in America. Make a list of the ways weather affects these families. Write an essay about how weather affects farming families and how we, as a society, can respond to the needs and demands of this part of the global society. (language arts standards 1 and 5)

4. Imagine you are a lobbyist for the rights of farmers. Read information on government subsidies. Determine whether government subsidies are or are not important. Plan a debate. (language arts standards 4 and 11)

5. Write a two-page creative work of a day in the life on the farm from the point of view of the rabbits on Jean Cadoret's farm. (language arts standard 5)

6. If your school has the organization Future Farmers of America, attend a meeting and interview a member. Write a short report on issues faced by farmers in your area. (language arts standard 11)

Social Studies Activities

1. Suppose you inherited a farm like Jean Cadoret's. Give reasons why you would or would not sell your farm. What would be your production plan? Where would you find water, and how would you ration it? Research prices and determine the amount of money you expect to receive for your vegetables and rabbits. Would you make enough money to maintain your farm? Would you make a profit? (social studies standard VII)

2. Jean Cadoret had little at his disposal for collecting and storing water. Research technologies available to Jean in the early 1900s in rural France. How would Jean's situation be different if he were living in the

present day? If present-day hydrotechnology had been available, would everyone in Provence accept and benefit from it? Devise a plan to bring present water source technologies to the countryside of Provence. (social studies standards III and VIII)

3. Research the geography of the countryside where Jean Cadoret's and Papet Soubeyran's farms were located. Make a map of the countryside, and include the relative positions of the two farms. Determine where you think the spring was located. Do you think one spring would have been sufficient to provide water for both farms? Draw a diagram of ways you would move water from the spring to the farms (social studies standards III, VII, and VIII)

4. Make a list of all the differences between Manon's experience growing up and yours. What are the common characteristics of the two cultures? (social studies standard I)

5. Explore the economic and personal effects of a drought (social studies standard III)

6. Read about divining rods. Compare the use of divining rods with technology used today to detect water sources. (social studies standard VIII)

Related Resources

Fiction

My Antonia by Willa Cather
O Pioneers! by Willa Cather
Out of the Dust by Karen Hesse
Angels in the Dust by Margot Theis Raven
Esperanza Rising by Pam Munoz Ryan
The Grapes of Wrath by John Steinbeck
Little House on the Prairie series, including *Farmer Boy*, by Laura Ingalls Wilder

Nonfiction

The Flower Farmer: An Organic Guide to Raising and Selling Cut Flowers by Lynn Byczynski and Robin Wimbiscus

Small-Scale Livestock Farming: A Grass-Based Approach for Health, Sustainability, and Profit by Carol Ekarius
The Divining Rod: A History of Water Witching by Arthur J. Ellis
Letters From the Dust Bowl by Caroline Henderson
Divining Rod: Its History, Truthfulness, and Practical Utility by Joseph Mullins and John Mullins
Successful Small-Scale Farming: An Organic Approach by Karl Schwenke and Ben Watson
Dust Bowl: The Southern Plains in the 1930s by Donald Worster

Websites

American Geological Institute (www.agiweb.org/earthcomm/) contains links to sites related to water and provides activities and resources for students. Includes charts, pictures, and photos. Also provides addresses of other related websites.

LIFE IS BEAUTIFUL

Grade Level: 6–12
Filmed: 1997 in color
Genre: Historical
Rating: PG-13
Time: 116 minutes
Language: Italian with some German
Director: Roberto Benigni
Theme: No greater love has any man than that he will lay down his life for another.
Interesting Facts: Filmed in Poland at Auschwitz, providing actual scenes from a real concentration camp, though the story itself takes place in an unnamed concentration camp in western Germany. The actor and actress playing Guido and Dora are married in real life.
Setting: The Italian countryside in prewar Italy and a German concentration camp in 1945, just weeks before the Americans arrive to liberate the camp.

Summary

The story begins in prewar Italy with a lighthearted account of the courtship of Guido and Dora, their marriage, and eventual birth of their son, Joshua. The family, even in time of war, is close-knit and happy until the day Dora arrives home to find her home in disarray and her husband and son missing.

Guido and Joshua, both Jewish, are taken to a Nazi concentration camp. Out of desperation to protect her son and join her husband, Dora, a gentile, voluntarily joins them. They are immediately separated and only see glimpses of each other when they first arrive at the camp.

Guido and his son, Joshua, are taken to a bleak, overcrowded dormitory where Guido immediately begins to shield his son from the horrors of life at the camp. He masterfully cares for his son while at the same time managing to survive the harsh working conditions in the camp. He fulfills his responsibilities with brilliance, compassion, and humor. The imaginative stories Guido invents to prevent his young son from knowing the truth of their circumstances are at once humorous and poignant.

Joshua, having little food to eat and noting that the other children have disappeared, wants to go home. Guido protects his son from certain death by creating a game of hide and seek, telling Joshua that the prize is a real tank. There are some beautiful moments when Guido finds ways to communicate with his wife. When the Americans liberate the camp, little Joshua, following the directions given to him by his father, remains hidden and wins the tank.

Characters

Guido: Ever-romantic male lead, views life with humor and optimism. He goes to great lengths to save his son from the horrors of a Nazi death camp.

Dora: Guido's faithful wife and mother of his son. She willingly goes to the concentration camp to avoid being separated from her family.

Joshua: Dora and Guido's five-year-old son. He thinks throughout the movie that his father took him on a vacation to a camp where they play games.

Uncle Eliseo: Guido's uncle and closest family member, who is taken to the concentration camp with the rest of the family.

Rodolpho: Banker and Dora's fiancé before she marries Guido. He refuses to sign Guido's request to open a bookstore.

Bartholomeo: Fellow prisoner at the concentration camp and friend of Guido.

Dr. Lessing: An old acquaintance of Guido and a physician at the concentration camp. He makes life a little easier for Guido by giving him a job as a waiter at the camp. He is obsessed with solving riddles.

Outline of Events

Prologue:

> This is a simple story, but not an easy one to tell.
>
> Like a fable, there is sorrow. And like a fable, it is full of wonder and happiness.

Part I: Life in Italy

1. The movie begins with light comedy in an Italian countryside. Guido frequently runs into a teacher, Dora, whom he calls Princess. He goes to great lengths to woo her and ultimately steals her away from her engagement party.

2. The following foreshadows of impending doom occur during this time:

a. Excessive bureaucratic requirements delay Guido's plans to open a bookstore.
b. German soldiers march in the streets.
c. Jewish slurs are written on buildings around town.
d. Businesses have signs forbidding Jews and dogs to enter.
e. Uncle Eliseo's horse is painted green with "Jewish horse" written on its side.

3. About six years pass; Guido and Dora have married and have a young son. Their life is happy and carefree in spite of the worsening discrimination against the Jewish people. Guido's small bookshop is adversely affected, having few customers because of the government's ban prohibiting gentiles from frequenting Jewish merchants.

4. On a fateful day, Germans come to the bookstore and order Guido to go with them for questioning. As he is led away he turns to look at Joshua,

winks, and walks with an exaggerated, humorous gait to amuse and reassure him. During the time Guido is gone, Dora's mother enters the bookstore and meets Joshua for the first time. Her anger over Dora's marriage to Guido dissolves after meeting Joshua. She tells him she will attend his birthday party the next day.

5. Dora picks up her mother and takes her to her home in anticipation of celebrating Joshua's birthday. Upon their arrival, Dora and her mother find the home in disarray—and Guido and Joshua are missing. Guido and Joshua, along with Uncle Eliseo and many of their neighbors, have been taken away by the Nazis and put on a train to a concentration camp. Dora, who is not Jewish, follows her family to the train station and convinces an uninterested German guard to let her be transported to the camp with her husband and child. Once at the camp the family is immediately separated into groups, male and female.

6. Several events that occurred early in the film arise again during the horrors of life in the prison camp, including Guido's optimism, humor, and daring; his training as a waiter; Dr. Lessing's riddles; an opera featuring "Barcarolle" from Offenbach's *Tales of Hoffman*; Joshua's lost toy tank; Joshua's adamant refusal to take a bath; and the family game of hide and seek.

Part II: Life in a German Concentration Camp

1. During the crowded and grueling truck and train ride to the concentration camp, Guido tells Joshua they are going on a special trip he planned for his birthday. To prevent his son from knowing the horrible truth of their situation, Guido makes each nightmarish event sound like a fun challenge.

2. After Joshua is separated from his mother and forced to live in subhuman conditions, Guido makes up a game of hide and seek. He provides his own humorous interpretation of the guard's harsh orders, telling Joshua that the guard is stating the rules of the game. Guido tells Joshua the guard has told them they can earn points toward winning first prize if they follow the rules. Joshua is never to say he is hungry, cry for his mommy, or be seen by the German guards. He must hide from the guards

by playing hide and seek. Each time Joshua follows the rules, he will earn points toward winning the first prize. Guido tells Joshua that once they earn 1,000 points, they will win a real tank.

3. Guido spots Dr. Lessing, the doctor who had been a friendly customer during the time Guido was a waiter in Italy. Dr. Lessing, now an officer in the German army, appears to have the power to help Guido and his family. Guido's hopes are dashed when he learns that the doctor just wants him to solve a riddle. The doctor, unconcerned about Guido and his family's plight, only wants to talk about how miserable he is because he cannot think of the answer to the riddle. Though the doctor does nothing to help Guido and his family escape the camp, he does give Guido a job as a waiter, a huge improvement from the harsh manual labor he had been doing.

4. Meanwhile, Joshua becomes tired of "the game" and states he no longer wants to win the tank. He begs his father to let him go home, but Guido convinces him to stay by telling him they are first on the points list, and if they go now, some other child will win the tank.

5. The war ends and there is mass chaos in the concentration camp. In their attempt to wipe out all evidence of the horrors and atrocities at the camp, the Germans engage in more mass killing. Guido frantically hides Joshua and then, dressing as a woman, tries to find Dora. He is caught in the process. Being led away by a German guard, Guido gives one last wink as he walks in an exaggerated, humorous gait past Joshua, who is watching his father from his hiding place.

6. Only when the shooting stops and silence begins, does little Joshua leave his hiding place. He is standing all alone in the middle of the camp when the roaring sound of a tank fills the air. Joshua's eyes light up when he sees his prize. A huge tank with an American flag stops right in front of Joshua and lets Joshua climb aboard. He has won first prize.

Epilogue:

> This is my story.
> This is the sacrifice my father made.
> This was his gift to me.

Vocabulary

A lengthy list of words and phrases from the subtitles of this film is provided. From this list teachers can choose the words most appropriate for their classes. Words appear in chronological order so they may be introduced and reviewed as needed.

brakes
explanation
landlady
urgent telegram
frightening
ingenuous
dangerous
apologize
omelet
magnificent surprise
farewell
congratulations
barbarians
Jewish store
silence
stubborn
invention
nightstand
velocipede (bike)
organization
madman
reservation
political views
mistake
bureaucratic procedure
first prize
signature
fabulous
complaint
coming through
substitute
hungry
scoundrel
thousand points
lobster/crustacean
loudspeaker
45 degree angle
lollipops
incredible
stomach ache
obscurity
hundred kilos
elementary school
obsessed
inspector from Rome
shower
theater
gas chamber
Race Manifesto (signed by Italian scientists)
anvils
superior
quick as lightning
Aryan
officials
perfection
cunning intelligence
movable cartilage
swarming
incredible
completely quiet

Before the Movie

1. Recall the times you have played hide and seek. What do you think the game hide and seek will have to do with the plot of the film?

2. Recall information you have learned about the Nazis and German concentration camps.

During the Movie

1. Why did Dora have to beg to be let on the train to the camp? Why wasn't she taken with her family?

2. If you were Dora, would you have willingly gone to a concentration camp?

3. What are the conditions at the concentration camp? What are some of the ways Guido is making conditions at the camp appear tolerable or even fun for Joshua?

After the Movie

1. Compare and contrast Guido's life before the war and during the war.

2. What sacrifices did Guido make for his wife? For his son?

3. Compare experiences of the other Jewish children in the concentration camp to the German children?

4. How did the movie remind you of other things you have read or seen about the Holocaust?

5. What was the function of comedy in the film?

Language Arts Activities

1. Visualize what life was like for Guido, Dora, or Joshua before, during, and/or after the war. Write about and/or illustrate the picture you have visualized. (language arts standards 2, 3, 5, and 6)

2. Visualize life in a concentration camp. Write a love note from Guido to Dora or from Dora to Guido. Describe how you will deliver your letter.

To set the mood, play "Barcarolle" from Offenbach's *Tales of Hoffman*. (language arts standard 2)

3. Find or develop other games Guido might have used to keep Joshua safe. Write the directions and include materials for your game(s). (language arts standard 12)

4. Study the Holocaust by going to the United States Holocaust Memorial Museum at www.ushmm.org to "A Learning Site for Students" (www.ushmm.org/outreach/index.html). (language arts standard 8)

Social Studies Activities

1. Find all the countries that were involved in World War II on a map. Label the countries that fought for the Allied and Axis powers. Calculate distances between and among the Allied and Axis countries. (social studies standard III)

2. Identify cultural aspects of life in Germany. Trace how German life changed from post–World War I through post–World War II. (social studies standard II)

3. When the movie began, the United States was not involved in World War II. However, at the end of the movie, the United States plays a significant role in Joshua's life. Research when and why the United States entered the war. (social studies standards II and VI)

4. What are some purposes of government? Describe the purpose of the German government after Hitler became chancellor in 1933. How did his leadership impact the dominant German population and minority groups? (social studies standard V)

Related Resources

Fiction

Terrible Things: An Allegory of the Holocaust by Eve Bunting
Stones in Water by Donna Jo Napoli
Four Perfect Pebbles: A Holocaust Story by Lila Perl
Holocaust Poetry by Hilda Schiff

Milkweed by Jerry Spinelli
Night by Elie Wiesel
War and Remembrance by Herman Wouk
Winds of War by Herman Wouk

Nonfiction

The Hiding Place by Corrie Ten Boom
The Diary of Anne Frank by Anne Frank
Daniel's Story by Carol Matas
Bearing Witness: Stories of the Holocaust by Hazel Rochman and Darlene Z. McCampbell
I Never Saw Another Butterfly: Children's Drawings and Poems From Terezin Concentration Camp, 1942–1944 by Hana Volavkova, editor

Music

"Barcarolle" from Offenbach's *Tales of Hoffman*

Game

Axis and Allies (Milton Bradley)

Website

The United States Holocaust Memorial Museum (www.ushmm.org) has sites for students, teachers, and families. Teaching materials and resources are available from this site.

M

Grade Level: 9–12
Time: 110 minutes
Filmed: 1931 in black and white
Language: German
Genre: True crime
Director: Fritz Lang
Rating: Not rated (some mild profanity)

Theme: Outrageous, hideous crime impassions us all.
Interesting Facts: This film is based on a true story about Peter Kurten, "the monster of Dusseldorf." The Nazis tried to halt the production of the film, believing the film was a metaphor about their movement.
This is the director's first "talking" film, having previously directed silent movies. Viewers are treated to the visual imagery used to communicate meaning in silent movies. Shadows, symbolism, and exaggerated human gestures accompany the spoken dialogue.
Setting: Berlin, Germany, in the early 1930s just prior to the rise of Nazi Germany. The film is in black and white, providing dark, haunting glimpses into the manhunt for a child killer.

Summary

The story is about a man driven by inner demons to abduct and kill little children. He has killed eight children before the movie begins. Through symbolism, not violence, the viewer knows when the killer has struck. Following the murder of the first on-screen victim, little Elsie Beckmann, hysteria erupts; people grow suspicious of anyone seen talking to children.

The child killings affect two distinct groups within the community: the police, who are working around the clock to solve the heinous crimes, and the criminals of the underworld—gangsters—who want the killer off the streets to diminish the increased presence of police in their neighborhoods. The street vendors, present on every corner of the city, are able to provide critical information about the whereabouts of the killer. The underworld criminals enlist their help to find the murderer. Scenes quickly alternate between meetings of the police and meetings of gang members. Much planning and action accompany the disparate groups' attempts to find and capture the child killer.

Once captured and subdued by the underworld and street vendors, they want to "crush him like a dog." They don't trust the police or the judicial system to keep him off the streets for long. The killer gives an impassioned plea for mercy, claiming that he can't help himself. The police arrive on the scene and arrest him. The ending is abrupt, leaving the viewer to wonder whether justice will be served.

M moves with persistence to tell a story that questions concepts of justice and retribution and why these concepts are so difficult to distinguish from one another.

Characters

Hans Beckert: Serial murderer of children in Berlin. He claims that he cannot help what he does to his victims.
Elsie Beckmann: The first on-screen murder victim.
Frau Beckmann: Mother of the murdered child, Elsie Beckmann.
Superintendent Löhmann: Head of the police force determined to find the murderer.
Schranker: Underworld leader. He decides members of the underworld must take matters into their own hands by finding the killer.
Franz: A member of the underworld who is tricked into telling the police the underworld's plans to capture the murderer.
Blind street vendor: Recognizes the tune Hans Beckert is whistling as he buys Elsie a balloon just before she is murdered.
Defense counsel: Defends Hans Beckert at an unlawful trial arranged by the underworld. He suggests that Hans Beckert is not responsible for his actions since he has no control over them.

Outline of Events

Part I: Introduction

1. *M* opens with a scene of children playing in the streets. They are innocently chanting the following childhood tune, foreshadowing imminent tragedy.

> Just you wait a while,
> The nasty man in black will come.
> With his little chopper,
> He will chop you up.

2. Frau Beckmann is waiting for her daughter, Elsie, to return home from school. She hears the children chanting and playing outside and becomes more anxious as time passes.

3. Elsie Beckmann, the first on-screen victim, is seen playing on her way home from school. She is innocently throwing her ball against one of the reward posters for the child killer when the shadow of the killer looms large over the poster. We see a few brief scenes of the killer and the little girl as he takes her for candy and a balloon. The stranger is whistling the tune "The Hall of the Mountain King" from Edvard Grieg's *Peer Gynt Suite* while he is with little Elsie. The passing of time and knowledge that a tragedy has befallen little Elsie are symbolized by a stark scene of a ball lying in the grass and a balloon caught in telephone wires.

4. The following day, the newspapers announce the murder of Elsie Beckmann. Within Berlin, a city of four million people, is a massive hunt for the child killer. Posters around the city offer a reward of 10,000 marks for the killer's capture. Police, sleeping only 12 hours a week, work around the clock to catch the killer. They profess to search every inch of the city, beginning with a radius of two kilometers around the scene of the last murder.

Part II: The Manhunt

1. Annoyed by the disruption of criminal activity caused by the police raids, the underworld leader calls a meeting to discuss plans to find the murderer themselves so they can continue their nefarious affairs uninterrupted. The underworld enlists the beggars' union to seek out and follow questionable characters.

2. With so much publicity and such close scrutiny of the comings and goings of the people of the city, neighbors begin to accuse each other of being the killer. Their accounts of what they see differ widely; one saw a man with a red hat, the other saw green.

3. While the underworld enlists the beggars' union for help in catching the murderer, the police begin to check up on recently released patients from asylums. They arrive at the apartment of a former mental patient, Hans Beckert, but he is not home. During the time the police are waiting for Hans Beckert to return, he continues to wander the streets. He encounters another little girl and offers to buy her a balloon. As he and the little girl approach the blind street merchant, Beckert is once again whistling "Hall of the Mountain King."

4. A break in the case occurs when the blind street merchant remembers hearing someone whistling a refrain from "Hall of the Mountain King" the day Elsie had been killed. He quickly calls to another street beggar to follow the man. The street beggar has a brilliant idea. Using chalk, he writes a large, thick letter *M* on his hand. He runs up to the suspect and pats him on the back, marking the back of the suspect with a big white *M*.

5. Unaware of the *M* on his back, Beckert continues walking with the little girl. The street people are able to follow him, guided by the big white *M*. Eventually the little girl sees the *M* and shows it to Beckert. He knows he has been detected and flees into a large building with many locked office stalls, thus sparing the little girl's life.

Part III: The Chase and Capture of the Child Killer

1. The race to find the killer is frantic; the underworld criminals and street people want to find him before the police arrive. The criminals tie up two night watchmen so they won't be able to call the police. One watchman eventually breaks free and immediately calls the police.

2. The underworld criminals and street vendors finally catch Hans Beckert, the killer, and hastily hold a trial in the cellar of the office building. They want to mete out their own brand of justice before the police arrive. During the trial Hans Beckert gives an impassioned plea for mercy, stating that he can't help what he does; he claims he is guided by irresistible impulses and shouldn't be punished for something he can't help. Just as the gang grows angry at his response and moves toward him to attack, the police arrive.

3. Beckert is apprehended by the police and tried in the court of law for the murders of the little girls. As the verdict is announced, the scene shifts to a bench occupied by the grieving mothers of the victims.

Vocabulary

A lengthy list of words and phrases from the subtitles of this film is provided. From this list teachers can choose the words most appropriate for their classes. Words appear in chronological order so they may be introduced and reviewed as needed.

murderer
vagrant
10,000 marks
underworld hangouts
victims
scruples
extra
systematic searches
evidence
beggars' union
danger
whistling
anxiety
watchmen
general public
don't walk like elephants
criminal
bunch of morons
slanderer
dubious honor
anonymous letter
mental impulse
outrage
irresistible impulse
fingerprints
invoke
indolent
pardon
insanity
wanderer
results
compulsive
headquarters
snuffed
homicide officers
asylum
radius of 2 kilometers
mercy
terrorizes the town

Before the Movie

1. What famous kidnapping cases can you recall? How do you think the kidnapper gained the trust of the victims? Discuss safety issues concerning walking or driving alone.

2. Knowing that some members in our society have unbalanced minds, what safety precautions should you take?

During the Movie

1. Discuss how people's lives changed because of the serial child killer.

2. Why do the children appear unafraid, even singing songs about the killer?

3. How would you react if you were a child at the time of the murders? What if you were a parent or teacher?

4. Discuss the role of the police in our society. What are some of the unexpected results of having a greatly increased police presence in the city?

5. How does the director use imagery to convey meaning?

After the Movie

1. The killer begged for mercy, saying he shouldn't be punished for something he couldn't help. What is your opinion of his plea? How should justice be served?

2. How do people with specific disabilities make contributions to society?

3. Based on the tone of the underworld criminals' dialogue, what was their attitude toward the children in the city and the child killer?

4. Describe the setting. How did the setting of an urban city contribute to the mood of the story?

Language Arts Activities

1. Explore aspects of the true crime genre. Determine the elements of story and setting used in the film that communicate the message. (language arts standard 2)

2. This story is centered around a tragedy that created a conflict among different groups in society. List and describe the characters and groups of people who were most affected by the tragedy. (language arts standard 2)

3. Why might the blind vendor be more apt to remember the tune the child killer was whistling than the other street people? Is the answer to this question expressed in the film? How did you determine your answer? What other facts were you able to determine based on the story, though not explicitly told to you. (language arts standard 3)

4. Imagine you are the blind street vendor. Describe your surroundings and experiences from the perspective of a person who is blind. What

senses will you most likely use to make sense of your world? Possible answers include the voices of children, the smell and feel of the grime of the streets, the smell and sound of the people who come to your stand, the sounds of footsteps, and music. (language arts standards 3 and 9)

Social Studies Activities

1. This story is based on a true story that took place in Germany in the 1920s. Peter Kurten, "the monster of Dusseldorf," was the real Hans Beckert. Research Peter Kurten and compare his life with the fictional life of Hans Beckert. Note: Many websites are available with information on Peter Kurten. Some contain graphic accounts of Kurten's lust for blood. You might want to print accounts suitable for your students rather than have them engage in an Internet search. (social studies standard IV)

2. *M* was released to the general public in Germany prior to the rise of the Nazi movement. Thinking the film was a thinly disguised portrayal of their group, Nazis tried to stop its release. They sent death threats to the director, causing him to leave Germany. To determine the concerns of the Nazis, list aspects of the criminal underworld's behavior and compare and contrast them with aspects of Nazi behavior. (social studies standards V and VI)

3. Describe the motivations of the police, the street vendors, and the underworld, whose work led to the capture of a killer. Which of the groups was working for the good of the community? (social studies standard V)

Related Resources

Fiction

In a Crooked Little House by A. G. Cascone
Missing! by Hannah Kuraoka
50 Greatest Mysteries of all Time by Otto Penzler
The Tell-Tale Heart by Edgar Allan Poe
The Last Goodie: A Novel by Stephen Schwandt
Dr. Jekyll and Mr. Hyde by Robert Louis Stevenson

Nonfiction

Serial Murder by Robert Dolan
The Lindbergh Baby Kidnapping in American History by Judith Edwards

Music

"Hall of the Mountain King" from Edvard Grieg's *Peer Gynt Suite*

THE MYSTERY OF KASPAR HAUSER

Grade Level: 9–12
Time: 110 minutes
Filmed: 1975
Language: German
Genre: Biographical drama
Director: Werner Herzog
Rating: Not rated (brief backside nudity)
Theme: Impacts of heredity and environment. What it means to be human.
Interesting Facts: Bruno S., the actor who plays Kaspar Hauser was himself a schizophrenic. He has much in common with Kaspar, having spent most of his formative years in institutions. The plot is based on a real-life story that took place in Nuremberg, Germany. At the time of Kaspar's death, some people doubted that there was an attacker, believing that Kaspar had attempted to gain attention by inflicting wounds on himself. Though never determined, some people thought Kaspar was born to a noble family.
Setting: The story begins in 1828 in a dark cellar outside of Nuremberg, where Kaspar has been held prisoner for 16 years. Most of the story is filmed in the city of Nuremberg.

Summary

This is a story of unthinkable human malevolence, anguished human spirit, and the overwhelming goodwill and sacrifice of ordinary citizens. The film opens with heart-wrenching scenes of a 16-year-old boy, Kaspar Hauser, chained in a cellar. His existence is meager; he consumes only the bread and water served to him. Since birth he has had no contact with the outside world and very little contact with his keeper, whom he calls Papa.

For unknown reasons, Kaspar is suddenly taken from his cell, exposing him to the outside world for the first time. When Kaspar is found, he becomes a curiosity among the townspeople. When they determine he is not dangerous, they offer friendship and help.

Two years later, Kaspar is still having serious problems adjusting to the world. He says, "People are like wolves to me." In spite of his problems, he is trying to make sense of the world. In response to a question from Count Stanhope, an English gentleman, about what it was like to live in a dark cellar, Kaspar replies, "Better than outside."

Issues of environment and heredity are clearly, though not explicitly, explored in this film. Kaspar learns to walk and talk, innate traits, remarkably quickly even though he has had little human contact. However, learning to play the piano, something he longs to do well, is difficult for him. Kaspar asks the question, "I can breathe; why can't I play the piano?" His ability to adapt and survive during his formative years was instinctual; his inability to make sense of the world is due to a lack of conditioning and prior experiences.

Kaspar has difficulty understanding traits and concepts of living and nonliving things. He ascribes human feelings to apples on the ground and is clearly puzzled when he asks how small people can build tall buildings. Throughout the film Kaspar is fascinated by other living things that are imprisoned or tethered, including a bird in a cage, a cow, a person living in a tower, and a baby in a bassinet.

Kaspar's advances in written and oral communication cause his original keeper, Papa, to take drastic steps to maintain the secret of his identify. To this day, no one has solved the mystery of Kaspar Hauser.

Characters

Kaspar Hauser: A young man without an identity, abandoned in the heart of Nuremberg. He has been abused and neglected since birth.

The keeper: Unnamed man who has held Kaspar prisoner in a dark cellar for 16 years and ultimately kills him.

The Rittmeister of the Fourth Squadron: The first person charged with the care of Kaspar after he is found abandoned in the middle of town.

Professor Daumer: Kindly older man who provides a home for Kaspar. He teaches Kaspar how to speak, write, and play the piano but is unable to teach him social skills.

Julius: A little boy who encourages Kaspar to talk.
Agnes: A little girl who tries to teach Kaspar a little German rhyme.
Pastor Fuhrmann: Local pastor who tries to help Kaspar find and understand God.
Count Stanhope: A noble gentleman who is interested in letting Kaspar live with him—until he sees his lack of social skills.
Scribe: A fusty old gentleman who is the scribe for the Rittmeister.

Outline of Events

1. Kaspar Hauser is seen chained in a cellar, passively playing with a little wooden horse. For 16 years, he has never experienced life outside the cellar. He has had very limited human contact and has been provided only with bread and water. Kaspar's only form of oral communication is through grunts and guttural noises. Kaspar's survival instinct is obvious by the way he attacks the bread and water he is given. He also appears interested in the rash and sores on his body.

2. For unknown reasons, the keeper suddenly removes Kaspar from the cellar, exposing him to the outside world for the first time. Supporting Kaspar in an upright position and urging him to walk, he brings Kaspar to the center of Nuremberg. Before abandoning him, he teaches Kaspar a single sentence to say to the people in town, "I want to be a gallant rider like my father was before me."

3. The keeper leaves Kaspar in the middle of a street, telling him to stay there and await his return. The keeper does not return; Kaspar is seen statue-like, patiently waiting and holding a note in one hand. The note says,

> From the Bavarian border, 1828
>
> His Excellency the Rittmeister. I'm sending your Gracye a boy. This here bouye wants to serve his Kinge faithfully. The bouye was layed on me 7th October 1812.
>
> I am a pore labourer with ten children and have enough to do to feed myself and my wife. His mother wanted to raise the boy, but I couldn't ask her to. I didn't tell her the boy was laid on me by the Court. I have not let him take one step out of the house since 1812 so nobody doesn't know a thing about him. You can ask him, but he can't tell you.

> I teached him reading and writing. And he says he wants to be a gallant ryder like his father was before him. If he had parents he would have been a smart fellow. You only have to show him something and he can do it. But please do not plie him with questions. He don't know where I am. I brout him away by night. I am not sining my name. [*Note:* This was translated with misspelled English words to represent the low educational level of the writer. Doubtless, the letter had many misspellings in German.]

4. One of the townspeople finds Kaspar, reads the note, and takes him to the Rittmeister's home. Not knowing what to do with him, the Rittmeister makes Kaspar spend the first night in his horse stall. Rittmeister and some of the townspeople have a difficult time waking Kaspar; he had been sleeping soundly in conditions not unlike the cellar where he had been imprisoned. Kaspar, lacking formal speech and social graces, shocks and dismays the townspeople.

5. The Rittmeister moves Kaspar to a locked room in a tower that is a prison for vagrants and criminals. Word has spread; Kaspar has become a curiosity. People who gather to watch him quickly determine he is not wild and begin to offer help and friendship.

6. One family invites Kaspar into their home and bathes him (brief backside nudity) and teaches him how to use a spoon. Kaspar finds food distasteful, and knowing no social skills, spits it out. When offered bread, he eats it willingly. Everyone, including the children, try to teach him to speak. Agnes, the little girl, tries to teach Kaspar this verse:

> Good morning little cat so white.
> May I sit down by your side?
> Be nice to me, little girl so fair.
> Then you may sit down right there.
> Lap, lap, lap,
> I like this milk.
> Lap, lap, lap
> As smooth as silk.

7. Kaspar reacts to events in surprising ways. A group of young delinquents maliciously scare him with a live chicken. However, when confronted with the real danger of a flame, Kaspar does not react. He touches

the flame; the pain causes him to cry, shedding tears without making a sound. Kaspar is fascinated by a little baby. He picks up a kitten and tries to make it walk on two feet as he does. During this time of exposure to the world, Kaspar makes a curious statement, "I am far away from everything."

8. As sympathetic as the townspeople are to Kaspar, he is becoming a financial burden. To earn money, they put him in a freak show at the circus. Kaspar is displayed as "the Foundling." Two other people are in the same show, "the Little King" and "Hombrecito the Flute Player." Kaspar's former keeper sees him and realizes he is learning to speak and may now identify him, thus setting the stage for future tragedy.

9. Kaspar and Hombrecito run away from the freak show. Professor Daumer finds Kaspar hiding in a shed and takes him to live at his house. While another guest, Florian, plays the piano, Kaspar listens to him carefully, saying, "The music feels strong in my heart." Puzzled as to why Florian can play the piano and he can't, Kaspar asks the question, "Why is everything so hard for me? Why can't I play the piano like I can breathe?"

10. When Kaspar returns to visit the tower, his first home in Nuremberg, he makes two interesting observations about the tower.

"A very, very big man must have built it. I would like to meet him." Professor Daumer replies that a man doesn't have to be as tall as the tower he builds.

"It can't be that I lived here. The room is only a few steps big. I don't understand. Whenever I look in the room to the right, to the left, frontwards, and backwards, there's only room. But when I look at the tower and I turn around, the tower is gone. So, the room is bigger than the tower!"

11. The townspeople worry that Kaspar does not have faith in God. He continues to confound them by his observations and lack of rational thought. Kaspar's lack of understanding of his world is dramatically shown when he sees green apples growing on a tree and red apples lying beneath the tree; he is told that the green apples will become red. Kaspar incredulously asks, "How do they do that?" Kaspar attributes human feelings and traits to the apples, saying they are smart apples. When

Daumer wants to move the apples, Kaspar says, "They are tired and want to sleep."

12. Kaspar begins to write his autobiography and is eager to learn more words. During this time he is invited to social events. One woman asks him what it was like to live in a dark cellar. Kaspar's reply: "Better than outside." When the pastor asks what he thought about in the cellar, he replies that he did not think of anything. When the townspeople take Kaspar to church, he says the singing of the congregation sounds awful, and when the singing stops, the pastor starts to howl. He says that he is only happy when he is in his bed.

13. Kaspar is sitting in a small shed. His keeper returns unexpectedly and clubs him. Kaspar's friends, following his bloody trail, find him and put him in bed. While in bed, Kaspar sees a vision of people climbing a mountain in very dense fog; it is very difficult for them to make the climb. When they reach their destination, they die.

14. Kaspar's keeper, learning that Kaspar is not dead, returns and stabs him. Kaspar's stepfather finds a note from the keeper on Kaspar that says "Hauser can tell you exactly what I look like and where I come from. To save him the trouble I'll tell you myself where I came from and even what my name is. M.L.O."

15. On his deathbed, surrounded by friends, the pastor, and a doctor, Kaspar tells a story about a caravan in the desert. He thanks everyone for listening to his story, then dies.

16. After his death, doctors perform an autopsy. They find that his cerebellum, the part of the brain that controls movement, is overdeveloped; the cerebrum, the part of the brain that controls thought and language, is underdeveloped. To this day, no one knows where Kaspar came from.

Vocabulary

A lengthy list of words and phrases from the subtitles of this film is provided. From this list teachers can choose the words most appropriate for their classes. Words appear in chronological order so they may be introduced and reviewed as needed.

murderer
horsey
dynasty
gallant rider
beyond reproach
fourth squadron
veritable mountain of fire
Rittmeister
scores (music)
Bavarian border
anonymous letter
signature
scaffold
passport
Sahara Desert
occupation
reasoning and deduce
police interrogation
haberdasher
refuses to answer
consumption (illness)
foundling
gout
blunt instrument
biography
prayer book
protégé
rosary
indescribable
mad or depraved
unsullied atmosphere
criminal or vagabond
bondage
berserk
caravan
empty
imagination
stomach
deformities
no conception of danger

Before the Movie

1. Study human development and man's dependence on human interaction. Contrast this with the development of familiar animals including dogs, cats, and birds.

2. Ask students to think how they learned to walk, talk, eat, and drink. What would their lives be like if no one taught them the skills of living and interacting with other people?

During the Movie

1. Ask students to predict whether they think Kaspar Hauser will ever live a normal life.

2. What skills will be the hardest for Kaspar to learn?

3. Discuss the role of the former keeper in Kaspar's development. Do you think Kaspar will meet up with his former keeper?

After the Movie

1. Discuss the following questions and observations made by Kaspar Hauser.

"How can a man make a tower higher than himself?"
"The room in the cellar is bigger than the tower."
"Women aren't good for anything but sitting still."
"Why are women allowed only to knit and cook?"
"How do they grow apples on trees?"

2. Discuss the morality of freak shows. Do they still exist today?

3. Why did the older boys try to scare Kaspar Hauser? How would adolescents react to someone like Kaspar Hauser today?

Language Arts Activities

1. Kaspar Hauser had begun writing an autobiography of his life. Pretend you are Kaspar Hauser. Write your autobiography. (language arts standards 5 and 12)

2. Imagine that Kaspar's keeper was tried for child abuse. Break into two teams, defense and prosecution. Using information from the film, including the keeper's final note, write opening and closing statements. Edit each other's work, looking for accuracy, clarity, persuasive language, and adequate descriptions. (language arts standards 5 and 6)

3. If Kaspar Hauser came face to face with his keeper, what would he say? Write a monologue of Kaspar Hauser expressing his feelings. Keep in mind that Kaspar is incapable of normal thinking. (language arts standard 5)

4. Illustrate Kaspar's dream about people struggling to climb a mountain and dying when they reach the top. Explain the meaning behind the

metaphor Kaspar used. Illustrate and write about other metaphors that would convey the same meaning. (language arts standards 3, 4, and 6)

Social Studies Activities

1. Analyze the impact of environment on human development, both physical and cognitive. (social studies standard IV)

2. Describe the impact of personality and physical disabilities on a person's ability to live a normal life. What would the impact be on the person's ability to be a good citizen? (social studies standards IV and X)

3. Create a timetable of human development, including speech, movement, and socialization. (social studies standard IV)

4. List the ways students learned to walk, talk, and play musical instruments. Ask how they learned to breathe, blink, and crave food and drink when they are hungry and thirsty. Separate answers into two categories: acquired skills and innate traits. (social studies standard IV)

5. Discuss the questions asked by Kaspar Hauser (see After the Movie, question 1, page 169). Illustrate ways Kaspar sought to understand his world. Did he seek to understand his roots or his past? Why or why not? (social studies standards I and IV)

Related Resources

Fiction

Tarzan of the Apes by Edgar Rice Burroughs
The Midwife's Apprentice by Karen Cushman
Where the Heart Is by Billie Letts
Z for Zachariah by Robert C. O'Brien
Island of the Blue Dolphins by Scott O'Dell

Nonfiction

Feral Children and Clever Animals: Reflections on Human Nature by Douglas Keith Candland

Wild Boy of Aveyron by Jean Marc Gaspard
Wild Boy of Aveyron by Harlan Lane
The Elephant Man: A Study in Human Dignity by Ashley Montagu and Trent Angus
Savage Girls and Wild Boys: History of Feral Children by Michael Newton
A Child Called "It": One Child's Courage to Survive by Dave Peltzer
The Lost Boy: A Foster Child's Search for the Love of a Family by Dave Peltzer
The Language Instinct: How the Mind Creates Language by Steven Pinker
The Forbidden Experiment: The Story of the Wild Boy of Aveyron, by Roger Shattuck and Douglas Keith Candland
The Elephant Man by Christine Sparks

RASHOMON

Grade level: 9–12
Time: 88 minutes
Filmed: 1950 in black and white
Language: Japanese
Genre: Drama
Director: Akira Kurosawa
Rating: Not rated (an off-screen rape occurs in this movie)
Theme: People describe events in ways that confirm previous strongly held beliefs.
Interesting Fact: An American version of *Rashomon*, *The Outrage,* was filmed in 1964.
Setting: Rashomon, the gate to the city of Kyoto and the surrounding Japanese countryside, in 12th-century Japan.

Summary

The story seeks to explain the murder of a man and the rape of his wife from the plausible but contradictory stories of four different people. During a torrential rainstorm, a priest, a woodcutter, and a common man take refuge under Rashomon, a large run-down gate at the entrance to Kyoto. They recount events from a murder trial, saying they have never heard anything so terrible. The woodcutter tells how he stumbled across a body of a man and ran to tell the police.

As the rain continues to fall, the priest and the woodcutter discuss three different versions of the crime told in court by the bandit (Tajomaru), the wife, and a medium who claims to speak for the husband. The commoner absorbs all that he is told of the accounts and questions the actions of each of the people involved. The woodcutter refutes one of the stories, leading the commoner to accuse him of knowing more than he has told. Later, the woodcutter's version adds yet another dimension to the crime.

The priest, after listening to the accounts, realizes that lies replaced the truth to preserve and enhance the witnesses' honor and reputations. He increasingly becomes despondent when he sees how easily the real honors of truthfulness and justice were abandoned to embrace a thin veneer of honor built on self-serving statements of lies and half truths. His faith in the goodness of the human soul, badly shaken by the accounts of the events, is redeemed at the end by an unrelated incident.

Characters

Tajomaru: Infamous bandit who may have murdered the nobleman.

Nobleman: Husband who is killed while accompanying his wife through the forest.

Wife: A beautiful woman married to a nobleman. She is allegedly raped by Tajomaru.

Firewood dealer (woodcutter): One of the four participants in the mysterious crime in the forest.

Priest: A member of the murder investigation. He is overwhelmed by the different versions of the crime.

Commoner: While waiting for the rain to stop, he listens to the priest's and woodcutter's tales. He is not disturbed by the murder because, as a skeptic, he believes nothing in the world is good. He believes that everybody lies in their own self-interest.

Medium: Summoned to speak as the nobleman to explain the events that led up to his death.

Policeman: Captured the bandit, Tajomaru, and brought him bound to the hearing.

Outline of Events

Part I: Introduction

1. A priest and a woodcutter wait under the Rashomon gate for the rain to stop. A commoner joins them. Noticing their somber mood, he asks what it is that bothers them. They explain that they have been at the courthouse listening to a murder trial. After hearing the events of the murder trial, the priest has begun to lose faith in the goodness of the human soul.

2. The priest and the woodcutter describe why they had to testify at the trial. The woodcutter came upon a woman's hat, a samurai's cap, a rope, an amulet, and a body when he was in the forest gathering wood. He immediately ran to the police to report what he had seen. The priest had been called to testify because he encountered the murdered man while traveling along the road three days earlier.

3. At the trial, the policeman who captured the bandit, Tajomaru, said he found him writhing by the banks of the river. The policeman had assumed the bandit had been thrown from the murdered man's horse. Tajomaru had the bow and arrows on his person, supposedly stolen from the murdered man, all evidence that he killed the nobleman.

Part II: Four Versions of the Same Crime

1. The bandit: Tajomaru exaggerates his own skill and bravery. He blames the entire event on "a little breeze." Here is his story. While sleeping under the shade of a tree, a breeze awakened him and he saw a beautiful woman. He had to have her! In an attempt to be alone with her, he tricked the husband into following him into the forest to find a treasure cache of swords, daggers, and mirrors. Deep in the woods, Tajomaru says he attacked the nobleman and bound him with rope. Then he returned to the woman, claiming her husband had been bitten by a snake. Frantic, she followed him and found her husband bound with a rope. Tajomaru attempted to rape the wife in front of her husband. At first she put up a fierce fight, trying to defend herself with a jeweled dagger, but he overpowered her. However, Tajomaru claims the wife quit struggling during the rape and began to enjoy it. He claims he had no intention of killing the husband afterward, but the wife, now having slept with two men, said only one

man could live. Tajomaru says he killed the husband in self-defense during a sword fight for her honor. After the death of her husband, the wife ran off, leaving her husband's sword behind. He had forgotten about the jeweled dagger.

2. The wife: The wife's tale is completely different from Tajomaru's story. Yes, she had been raped in front of her poor husband, who had been tied to a tree. After the rape, Tajomaru untied her husband, sneered at them both, and left. Sobbing, the wife ran to her husband and lay prostrate at his feet, begging forgiveness. However, she claims to have seen cold hatred, not compassion, in her husband's eyes. She begged her husband, "Don't look at me like that. Don't look like that." Seeing his loathing, she begged him to kill her. The wife fainted, and when she came to, her husband was dead.

3. The husband: A medium is summoned as the third witness. Through the medium, the husband recounts his story. He begins by saying, "I am in darkness now. I am suffering in darkness. Cursed be those who cast me into this hell of darkness." He tells the story of his beautiful wife being attacked by the bandit while he was helplessly tied to a tree. After the attack, he was stunned when his wife told the bandit to take her with him and kill her husband. Instead, Tajomaru freed him before leaving with his wife. Grieving, he kills himself with his wife's jeweled dagger. The medium describes the scene after his death:

> Everything was quiet.
> A mist seemed to envelop me as I lay quietly in the shadows.
> Someone was approaching,
> Softly, gently.
> Who could it have been?
> Then a hand grasped the dagger and drew it out.

4. The woodcutter: On hearing the medium's account, the woodcutter blurts out, "That's not true!" The commoner finally understands; he knows the woodcutter did not tell the whole story. He confronts the woodcutter, declaring that he must have seen it all. The woodcutter reluctantly tells his story, claiming he kept quiet because he did not want to become involved. He says he came upon the woman, who was desperately crying,

her husband tied to a tree. The bandit was on his knees begging the woman to go with him. He offered to give up being a bandit and work hard to live an honest life. When the woman refused, he threatened to kill her. She freed her husband, who turned on her, calling her a "shameless whore." The wife's pitiful crying turned to mocking laughter as she accused both men of being weak. She goaded them into a sword fight by saying their manliness could only be determined by the strength of swords. The men reluctantly and clumsily fight. Through sheer luck, the bandit kills the nobleman. The bandit, rebuffed again by the wife, runs away.

Part III: Redemption at Rashomon Gate

1. Back at Rashomon gate, all the stories have been told. The skeptic asks the priest which of the stories he believes. During this time a baby's cry is heard. In a corner, the commoner finds an abandoned infant and takes the swaddling clothes wrapped around the baby. The woodcutter is angry that the commoner would do such a thing to a child. The commoner tells the woodcutter he too is not so honorable and accuses him of stealing the jeweled dagger from the dead man.

2. The priest, disillusioned and devastated by the dishonesty of humankind, regains his faith in basic human goodness when the woodcutter offers to take the infant into his care. Outside, the rain stops and the sun begins to shine.

Vocabulary

A lengthy list of words and phrases from the subtitles of this film is provided. From this list teachers can choose the words most appropriate for their classes. Words appear in chronological order so they may be introduced and reviewed as needed.

what's wrong
swords, daggers, mirrors
understand
jealous
strange
determined

prison courtyard
disgraced
murdered
inlay
earthquake
sneered

famine
struggled
plague
fainted
disasters
confused
bandits descend upon us
console
horrible
cunning
epidemics
pitiless words
testify
farce
I swear to it
amulet
life is delicate
suspicious
fleeting as the morning dew
ashamed
retribution
grateful
glimpse

Before the Movie

1. Think of a time that the recounting of a serious event was distorted. Did versions of the event differ from one another?

2. Why do you think people distort the truth? Give some examples.

During the Movie

1. Consider the principal characters: the husband, wife, bandit, and woodcutter. Whose story seems most believable?

2. Why do you think the priest and the woodcutter thought the events in the forest were so terrible, worse than earthquakes and the plague?

3. The woodcutter will be called upon to give a version of events concerning the rape of the wife and the killing of her husband. Predict how his account of events will vary from the preceding accounts.

After the Movie

1. Do you think the director intended for us to know the truth about the man and the woman? What do you think is the main message of the story?

2. What was the significance of the abandoned baby to the story?

Language Arts Activities

1. Compare the stories of the husband, wife, bandit, and woodcutter. Determine a common theme throughout the stories. (language arts standards 1, 2, and 3)

2. Compare the stories of the wife, husband, bandit, and woodcutter. Determine the motives each person had for intentionally distorting the events. (language arts standards 3 and 6)

3. Based on the woodcutter's account, none of the principle characters acted honorably, including himself. To illustrate the difference one person's actions can make in the lives of others, choose a character and predict what might have happened if that character's actions had been honorable. (language arts standards 2 and 3)

4. Read accounts of other cultures from the 12th century. List and describe how honor was defended in other cultures.(language arts standards 1, 7, and 9)

Social Studies Activities

1. Think of a serious event from your personal lives or the news. Listen to the accounts of the event from several people and determine how the accounts differ. Look for evidence of bias, and determine possible underlying motives for the bias. (social studies standard IV)

2. Many of the tragic actions in the film occurred because of honor. Men felt they had to defend their own honor as well as the honor of a woman. Women felt they lost their honor if they had been with more than one man. Compare the differences in morality between 12th-century Japan and today. (social studies standards I, II, and IV)

3. People exhibit many of the same traits, unchanged by time and place. Look for examples of human behavior that are the same today as they were in 12th-century Japan. (social studies standard I)

4. Write a report responding favorably or unfavorably about the use of fighting and killing as a cultural response for defending one's honor. (social studies standard I)

Related Resources

Fiction

Rashomon and Other Stories by Ryunosuke Akutagawa
Rashomon Gate by I. J. Parker

Nonfiction

Telling Yourself the Truth by William Backus and Marie Chapian
Telling the Truth by Lynne V. Cheney

SEVEN SAMURAI

Grade Level: 6–12 **Time:** 204 minutes
Filmed: 1954 in black and white **Language:** Japanese
Genre: Epic history **Director:** Akira Kurasawa
Rating: Not rated (bloodless violence and thonged backsides of men)
Theme: One man with courage makes a majority.
Interesting Fact: *The Magnificent Seven*, filmed in 1960, is a Hollywood western based on the film *Seven Samurai*.
Setting: Early 16th-century Japan, where civil war led to chaos and lawlessness. Most of the action takes place in and around a poor farming village that has been repeatedly looted by bandits at harvest time.

Summary

The opening line of the film clearly describes the plight of people trying to exist in a lawless nation: "In the early 16th century, Japan was in the throes of civil wars and farmers everywhere were being crushed under the iron heels of cruel bandits."

Bandits have recently raided a small farming village, looting, burning, killing men, and kidnapping women. Crops were either stolen or destroyed, leaving the survivors grieving and without hope. With their crops plundered, there is no income to pay for security. One of the farmers sadly proclaims, "Farmers are born to suffer. That's our lot."

With an almost childlike acceptance, they anticipate repeated lootings and a life of suffering.

Few leaders exist in the village. Their ideas are met with little help or encouragement from the rest of the villagers. One young farmer, Rikichi, attempts to convince the other men in the village to find a way to fight the bandits. Having no money, they decide to look for hungry samurai willing to work for food.

Kambei is the first samurai recruited. Peace for the villagers depends on whether he can recruit other samurai to support his mission. Once seven samurai are found, they work to train the villagers to fight off the bandits, no easy task considering the hysteria and hopelessness shown by the men in the village.

During their time together, the samurai become a close-knit band of fighters, grieving deeply when one of their own is killed. In the end the sacrifice among them is high; four of the seven samurai are killed. Child-like, the people in the village have returned to their daily work, oblivious to the samurai who had given them so much. The surviving samurai, no longer needed by the village people, are the only ones grieving for their fallen friends.

Characters

Kambei Shimada: A noble ronin, the first samurai recruited by the village people. He helps recruit six other samurai.

Katsushiro Okamoto: The youngest samurai and disciple of Kambei. He falls in love with farmer Manzo's daughter, Shino.

Gorobei Katayama: Wise samurai praised by Katsushiro for his skill and humility.

Heihachi: Cheerful samurai, a fencer from the woodcut school.

Kyuzo: Samurai, a master swordsman.

Shichiroji: Samurai and longtime friend of Kambei.

Kikuchiyo: Poses as a samurai. He is an impulsive and frenetic son of a murdered farming family.

Farmer Rikichi: A young farmer who tries to rally the villagers to take steps to protect themselves. Unbeknownst to the samurai or the village people, his wife is kidnapped by the bandits and kept prisoner in a hut nearby.

Farmer Manzo: Obsessed father, certain that his daughter, Shino, will be defiled by the samurai.
Farmer Yohei: A timid, nervous man. His job is to guard the rice that is reserved for the seven samurai.
Grandad (sic): Patriarch of the farmers. He proposes the idea of hiring samurai to defend the village.

Outline of Events

Part I: The Samurai

1. A small village in rural Japan has been the target of numerous raids by bandits. Bandits have stolen their crops and some of the women, leaving total devastation behind them. The farmers have replanted their fields and are expecting to harvest their first crop in two weeks. They fear that the bandits will once again return.

2. The villagers' fears are founded. The bandits are planning to loot the village after the barley has ripened. Nearby, Farmer Yohei overhears this tragic news and alerts the town of the looming attack. Villagers, with intense feelings of fear and hopelessness, are reduced to hand-wringing and wailing.

3. Farmer Rikichi tries to rouse the other farmers into action. They consult the village elder, Grandad, who tells them that he saw with his own eyes villages that had been spared because they were protected by samurai. He advises the farmers to hire hungry samurai who are willing to work for food.

4. Rikichi organizes some men from the village to walk to a nearby city and look for seven out-of-work and hungry samurai. The mission is carried out with urgency because the barley has ripened, and the villagers fear the bandits will return at any time. Using food as an incentive, Kambei auditions a round of samurai using various techniques to test the agility and alertness of each man.

5. The village men recruit six samurai, Kambei, Katsushiro, Shichiroji, Heihachi, Gorobei, and Kyuzo. The seventh man, Kikuchiyo, is a farmer posing as a samurai. He arrives at the samurai's hut in a drunken state,

loud and obnoxious. The samurai catch him in a lie about his background but are intrigued by his forceful, wild spirit and accept him. Thus, seven samurai return to the village.

6. The village people are fearful about having the samurai near their daughters. Farmer Manzo forcibly cuts his daughter Shino's hair and demands that she wear men's clothes so she will be mistaken for a boy.

7. The villagers hide from the samurai, terrified they will take advantage of the women. To expose their hypocrisy, Kikuchiyo sounds a false alarm indicating bandits have been spotted. The villagers rush outside of their homes in a panic, beseeching the newly arrived samurai to protect them.

8. The samurai commence to make plans for the imminent attack. Kambei scouts several vulnerable parts of the village and suggests ways to fortify them. Other samurai lead men in battle training sessions, using cheers to rally morale. Katsushiro comes upon Shino, dressed like a boy, picking flowers. She runs away and he follows her, discovering that she is, in fact, a girl.

9. The samurai are unaware that people in the village are starving. The village people, having given their rice to the samurai to pay for protection, exist on millet. Katsushiro, upon tasting millet for the first time, is disgusted and gives his portion of rice to Shino. Shino, in turn, gives her rice to an old woman almost dead from starvation.

10. With the crops ready for harvest, the bandit attack is imminent. Outlying compounds cannot be saved from the attack, and villagers are instructed to convene in the heart of the village to build barricades and finish training for battle.

11. Attracted to each other, Shino and Katsushiro take a walk in the woods, where they encounter scouts from the bandits. Katsushiro alerts the samurai, and they discuss attacking the bandits' fortress to reduce the number of bandits who will reach the farming village.

Part II: The Defense of the Village

1. During the battle preparations, life is remarkably normal. The villagers have been lulled into complacency by the recent peaceful times.

Women who had remained hidden since the samurai arrived come out to harvest crops; the samurai, seeing the women for the first time, engage in antics to impress them.

2. Seeing that the villagers are no longer concerned about the bandits, the samurai say that now is the time for maximum alert, not passiveness. Going on the offensive, they plan an attack on the bandits' camp.

3. During this time of planning, the samurai tell Rikichi he would be more productive if he were married. Rikichi runs off to be alone. Concerned, the samurai find him and unsuccessfully try to get him to talk about what is bothering him.

4. The samurai attack the bandits' fortress in a surprise raid. During this time, they learn Rikichi's painful secret. Rikichi sees his kidnapped wife fleeing from a burning building and attempts to run to her. When Heihachi, the happy samurai, goes to help Rikichi, he is killed.

5. During Heihachi's funeral the bandits attack the village. Kikuchiyo encounters a fatally injured mother carrying a baby away from the burning mill. She dies immediately after handing the baby to him. Kikuchiyo is overcome with grief, saying that the same thing happened to his family when he was a baby. Grandad, who had said he wanted to die in the mill, perishes in the fire. The elaborate preparations, motivated by the samurai, stop the bandits from penetrating the main part of the village, and the bandits are forced to retreat.

6. The battle resumes at night. Kambei keeps a tally by crossing off circles representing bandits each time a bandit is killed. He plans on decreasing the number of bandits one by one.

7. In the morning the villagers use a scarecrow to draw fire. They have a plan to let the bandits in a few at a time and methodically eliminate them one at a time. Kikuchiyo, disguising himself as a bandit, leaves his post and attacks one of the bandits and steals his gun. His feat is not considered brave by the samurai, but instead pretentious. His mischief invites more bandits. During the ensuing battle, Gorobei is killed.

8. On the eve of the third and decisive battle, Shino and Katsushiro consummate their love for one another. Shino's father is outraged by his

daughter's betrayal of honor. In a lengthy scene, he beats and chastises her in front of the village people and the samurai.

9. The next day, the largest and last battle begins under the veil of heavy rain. The villagers defeat the last of the bandits, but at a high cost. Two more samurai are killed; only Kambei, Shichiroji, and Katsushiro are left.

10. While the samurai walk past the four graves of their fellow warriors, the villagers ignore them, showing total disregard for their sacrifices that enable them to live in peace. The samurai hear the villagers singing as they alone grieve for their friends.

Vocabulary

A lengthy list of words and phrases from the subtitles of this film is provided. From this list teachers can choose the words most appropriate for their classes. Words appear in chronological order so they may be introduced and reviewed as needed.

village lips are tightly shut like a bolted door
forced labor
suffering
drought
bottled up
bandits
thrashing
stop complaining
wretched
magistrate
peasant
bamboo spears
it's evident
impossibility
prisoner of war
negotiate
avenge son's death
insolence
deploy
millet
mollycoddles
daughter
wry face
priest
dissention (alternate way to spell *dissension*)
disciple
sentries
ronin (out-of-work samurai)
decisive battle
overestimate
band of forty bandits
meager meals
intolerable
outrageous
square meal
terrified

fed up with fighting
splendid principle
prowess
warlord
hospitality
patriarch
harvest
plague
splendid scarecrow

Before the Movie

Note: Because of the unfamiliar spelling of Japanese names, it would be helpful to list and review the names before showing the film. To demystify the names, provide students with a list of the characters.

1. Discuss crime in your area. How do you protect yourselves from crime?

2. What if there were no police? How would you be responsible for your own law and order?

3. What traits would you look for when seeking someone to defend you?

During the Movie

1. Discuss the personalities of the individual samurai. What are their reasons for fighting for the village? Are their reasons the same or different? Make a list of the seven samurai to use as a reference while viewing the rest of the movie.

2. What are some of the humanitarian acts shown by the samurai?

After the Movie

1. Describe the tactics used by the samurai to defeat the bandits.

2. What was the attitude of the village people toward the samurai after the defeat of the bandits? Recall instances where the attitudes of the village people toward the samurai might be mirrored by people today.

Language Arts Activities

1. As a class, discuss the problems faced by the village. Besides hiring samurai, what other options do you think the villagers could have em-

ployed to keep their village safe? Write a Village Protection Plan and present it to the class. (language arts standards 4, 5, and 7)

2. *Seven Samurai* offers discourse about human interaction, class systems, concepts of honor, and the importance of teamwork. Choose one of the principles and write a report on the way it impacts your life today. Discuss your ideas. (language arts standards 5 and 6)

3. One of the 16th-century Japanese farmers wails, "Farmers are born to suffer. That's our lot," upon hearing the bandits are planning another attack. Research present-day farming in the United States. What problems do farmers today encounter? How are their problems different from the 16th-century Japanese farmers? After reading about farming in the United States, explain whether you agree with the statement "Farmers are born to suffer." (language arts standards 7 and 8)

Social Studies Activities

1. Research the history of law enforcement agencies. What are their purposes? Compare the needs for law enforcement of the citizens in 16th-century Japan with needs of the American colonists. Note any similarities and differences. (social studies standards V and X)

2. While *Seven Samurai* is a deeply emotional film, it is also a careful depiction of culture and time. In groups, compare the culture of 16th-century Japan with our culture today. Analyze similarities and differences in the roles and duties of individual citizens, technology, structures of power, and economic demands. (social studies standards I, VI, and VII)

3. The samurai drew a map of the village. They used the map for making their battle plans. The village in the film is located in a valley surrounded by mountains next to a stream. Divide the class into groups. Research the geography, including the topography of Japan. Create a map of a small village. From this map, devise a plan for defense against marauding bandits. (social studies standard III)

4. The samurai had a code of behavior. Read about the code of behavior of groups present in our society today (Girl Scouts and Boy Scouts, military, police, educators). Compare the code of behavior of the samurai and a group present in our society. (social studies standards V and X)

5. The citizens in the village were left to govern themselves. There appeared to be no centralized power of government. Discuss the pros and cons of a centralized power of government. (social studies standard VI)

Related Resources

Fiction

Forty-Seven Ronin Story by John Allyn
The Boy and the Samurai by Erik C. Haugaard
The Revenge of the Forty-Seven Samurai by Erik C. Haugaard
The Samurai's Tale by Erik C. Haugaard
Sword of the Samurai: Adventure Stories From Japan by Eric Kimmel
The Sign of the Chrysanthemum by Katherine Paterson

Nonfiction

Samurai: An Illustrated History by Mitsuo Kure
Code of the Samurai by Tracey West

UMBRELLAS OF CHERBOURG

Grade Level: 9–12
Filmed: 1964 in color
Genre: Musical love story
Time: 91 minutes
Language: French
Director: Jacques Demy
Rating: Not rated
Theme: Change and growth are inevitable.
Interesting Fact: The entire dialogue during the film is set to music.
Setting: Cherbourg, a deep-water port on the Normandy peninsula in northern France. The story spans a six-year period during Algeria's war of independence against France, beginning in 1957.

Summary

Seventeen-year-old Geneviève is ready to experience life outside her mother's umbrella shop. She has fallen in love with a mechanic named Guy and is ecstatic—until her mother finds out. Everything goes downhill from there. When Guy is drafted into the French army to fight against Algeria in its war of independence from France, Geneviève finds out she is pregnant. Her mother, seeking to help Geneviève while also helping her own financial situation, encourages her to marry a wealthy suitor. This is a tale of star-crossed lovers and missed opportunities. Guy returns from the war to find that Geneviève has not waited for him and has married another. He is devastated, but eventually a longtime friend of the family pulls him out of his depression. It isn't until Geneviève and Guy have both married others and had children that they see each other again. The movie poses questions about life and life choices.

Characters

Guy Foucher: The 20-year-old boyfriend of Geneviève; he dreams of owning his own service station but is first drafted into the French army.
Geneviève: The 17-year-old girlfriend of Guy; she works for her mother in the umbrella store.
Élise: Guy's godmother who has raised him since he was little. She is now elderly and bedridden.
Madeleine: A family friend and caretaker of Guy's bedridden godmother. She is secretly in love with Guy.
Madame Emery: Geneviève's mother. She owns an umbrella shop and is opposed to her daughter falling in love at the tender age of 17.
Monsieur Doubourg: The jeweler in whose store the Emerys meet Roland Cassard.
Roland Cassard: Wealthy suitor and eventual husband of Geneviève.
Françoise: The young daughter of Geneviève and Guy; the adopted daughter of Roland.
François: Guy and Madeleine's young son.

Outline of Events

Part I: The Departure

1. Geneviève and Guy are young, carefree, and madly in love. Guy is working as an auto mechanic, and Geneviève works in her mother's umbrella shop. The young lovers dream of a life together and plan to marry.

2. Before Guy and Geneviève can fulfill their dreams, fate intervenes. Guy is drafted into the French army. Geneviève begs him not to go. She claims she cannot live without him.

3. They tearfully part, promising their undying love for each other.

Part II: The Absence

1. Guy leaves for the Army. He is leaving behind a tearful Geneviève; his ailing godmother, Élise; and her caregiver, Madeleine.

2. Geneviève keeps busy helping her mother in her umbrella store. During this time she learns she is pregnant with Guy's baby; she is desperate to hear from Guy, whose letters are infrequent.

3. Geneviève's mother is struggling financially and in danger of losing her umbrella shop. She seeks help from a wealthy gem dealer, Mr. Cassard.

4. Mr. Cassard takes an interest in Geneviève and asks her to marry him. Geneviève, discouraged because she has not heard from Guy, and desperate because of her pregnancy, accepts his proposal. Thinking she may never see Guy again, she and Mr. Cassard marry.

Part III: The Return

1. Guy returns home after being hospitalized with a leg injury he received during the war. He is hit with the news of Geneviève's marriage and his godmother's death. Dispirited and discouraged, Guy is comforted by his godmother's caretaker, Madeleine.

2. Madeleine is in love with Guy, and with patience and time, he falls in love with her. They marry and have a child. With his inheritance from his godmother, Guy fulfills his dream of buying a service station. Life is good.

3. During Christmas time, Geneviève, seeing the sign in Guy's gas station, stops to talk to him. There is polite conversation, but Guy makes no effort to reestablish a relationship with Geneviève, even though she has had his child.

4. Geneviève leaves and almost immediately Guy's wife and son return from Christmas shopping. The movie ends with a Norman Rockwell–style scene of Guy and his family hugging one another and playing in a snowy landscape, illuminated by the lights of the gas station.

Vocabulary

A lengthy list of words and phrases from the subtitles of this film is provided. From this list teachers can choose the words most appropriate for their classes. Words appear in chronological order so they may be introduced and reviewed as needed.

ignition
jewels
Mercedes
emergency
overtime
atrocious
gasoline
savior
perfume
philanthropist
customer
draft notice
theater
Algeria
umbrella
dangerous
none of your business
separation is cruel
coward
prescription
gas station
pregnant
marriage
Antwerp
flabbergasted
broach a subject
godmother
preoccupied
exaggerate
Amsterdam
seize our property
furlough
it is out of the question
carnival
francs
hospital
live modestly
maneuvers
hand grenades

Before the Movie

1. What do you like about listening to rap or pop music? Have you ever tried to communicate just by singing? This film is all in song.

2. To set the mood for a story told through song, sing directions and other information you wish to communicate to the students. Model a few lines and then let the students try.

3. Have you ever been in love? If so, how did you feel when you had to be separated? Did you think you would wait forever? What might cause you to find someone else?

4. Look for an example of irony during the first part of the film. (Guy and his friends, while grooming themselves before a date to the movies, complain that they find it boring to watch movies with singing.)

During the Movie

1. How does the singing affect your enjoyment and understanding of the film?

2. Why must Guy go to war?

3. What do you think will happen during the time Guy is away?

4. Do you think Guy and Geneviève will get married?

After the Movie

1. How much time passed from the beginning to the end of the movie?

2. Why do you think Madeleine was so quiet at first?

3. What was Roland's occupation, and why was this better in Mrs. Emery's eyes than Guy's occupation?

4. Should Guy have made an effort to meet his child by Geneviève?

5. Did you like the ending? Why or why not?

6. What was the purpose of the singing? Did you like it?

7. Note: If students enjoyed this musical film, they might enjoy the film *Beauty and the Beast* shown with the accompanying opera *La Belle et la Bête*, written by Philip Glass. The soundtrack from the film can be turned down and replaced by Glass's opera, which he synchronized with the plot.

Language Arts Activities

1. After Guy left for Algeria, the only way for him and Geneviève to communicate was through letters. Write a letter to someone in the U.S.

military who is on duty. Get the address information from local or state military bases. (language arts standards 5 and 6)

2. If Guy and Geneviève were to be separated during the present day, what types of communication would be available to them? (language arts standard 8)

3. Think about people who are at war or are away from their loved ones because of duties. Write a diary either from the perspective of the soldier or someone left behind at home. (language arts standards 5 and 6)

4. Choose a scene from the movie and rewrite it so that it fits modern-day American culture. Perform the new creation, noting cultural differences and similarities. (language arts standards 4, 5, and 6)

Social Studies Activities

1. Mrs. Emery's umbrella shop was not very profitable. Think of reasons for her lack of profit. Plan ways to improve the shop. What else could be sold in an umbrella shop that might attract buyers? Come up with a business plan to boost sales and increase Mrs. Emery's profit. (social studies standard VII)

2. Check locations of umbrella manufacturers. Which locations of manufacturers would most likely be cost-effective for importing or sending umbrellas to Cherbourg, France? How could the umbrellas be sent? What would be the estimated time for receiving the umbrellas? (social studies standards III and VII)

3. How did soldiers in the French national army differ from soldiers in the French Foreign Legion. What is a mercenary? What is a soldier of fortune? Determine whether there is an ethical difference between the soldiers in the French Foreign Legion and the French national army. (social studies standard V)

4. An Algerian uprising against France was the reason Guy had to go to war. Research the history of France between 1945 and 1959. What other countries broke colonial ties with France? Draw a map of France and its colonies. Create a timeline showing when each colony broke away from

France. Explain the reasons behind the indigenous people's opposition to France. (social studies standards III and IV)

5. What was the outcome of the war with Algeria? How did the outcome affect the French people? (social studies standards IV and VI)

6. When Charles de Gaulle became president of France in 1958, he was instrumental in writing a new constitution, one that gave more power to the president. Compare the French constitution before 1958 with the one written in 1958. Compare the new French constitution with the Constitution of the United States. (social studies standards II and VI)

7. After Vietnam, Laos, and Cambodia broke colonial ties with France, between 1945 and 1954, the Vietnam War broke out. Determine whether the newly acquired independence of each of these nations led to the Vietnam War. List and discuss probable causes for the unrest and fighting that occurred in these nations. (social studies standard IX)

8. French control of Vietnam, Laos, and Cambodia was loosened by the post–World War II insurgency of Vietnamese leaders such as Ho Chi Minh. The French control collapsed completely after the decisive battle at Dien Bien Phu in 1954. How do these events relate to the American experience in Vietnam in the 1960s? (social studies standard IX)

Related Resources

Fiction

Wuthering Heights by Emily Brontë
The Everlasting Covenant by Robyn Carr
Gone With the Wind by Margaret Mitchell

Nonfiction

Life in the French Foreign Legion: How to Join and What to Expect When You Get There by Evan McGorman
The French Foreign Legion: A Complete History of the Legendary Fighting Force by Douglas Porch

Music

Soundtrack to *Umbrellas of Cherbourg* by Michel Legrand

WAR AND PEACE, PART I

Grade Level: 9–12
Time: 140 minutes
Filmed: 1968 in color
Language: Russian and French
Genre: Epic history
Director: Sergei Bondarchuk
Rating: Not rated
Theme: Tragedy and happiness coexist in the human condition.
Interesting Facts: This epic film is based on the book by Leo Tolstoy. He created composite characters from friends and acquaintances.
In 1968 the film cost $100 million to make.
Setting: St. Petersburg, Russia, 1805, during the Napoleonic Wars. Scenes of palaces, grand salons, the Russian countryside, and battlefields richly portray Russian life during the reign of the tsars.

Summary

This story is a juxtaposition of frivolity, natural death, and war; all are part of the human experience. "I simply cannot understand why men cannot live without war" exemplifies the thinking of the women at that time. Most men consider it their duty and honor to fight for their motherland. One man, Pierre, is caught between the world of high society and war. Being an illegitimate son of a count, Pierre has grown up without a vision for his life, always questioning and searching for his place. Andrei, a Russian officer and Pierre's best friend, is a typical member of the nobility, desirous of serving his country during the time of war.

Two separate stories, war and peace, detail vivid and colorful accounts of Russian life. The story begins at an opulent party in a grand salon, where Russian officers and their women discuss politics and war. Women, quiet supporters of their husbands, talk about life as they know it, fearful of the changes that are to come. Princess Lisa, pregnant with Andrei's baby, is one of many women who are left behind to cope with life while their husbands are gone.

Battle scenes between the Russo-Austrian army and Napoleon at Austerlitz are majestic. The colors, music, and seemingly choreographed battle scenes show clearly how armies fought in the 1800s. Soldiers on both sides, dressed in colorful uniforms, advance in columns. Rifles in 1805 were capable of shooting only a single round. Therefore, soldiers advanced, shot at their targets, and stepped backward to reload while the second rank advanced and fired.

During the battle of Austerlitz, Andrei is wounded and eventually arrives home. Upon his arrival he is greeted by his jubilant sister and father, who feared he had been killed in the war. Tragically, his wife, Princess Lisa, suffering a long and excruciating labor, does not comprehend that Andrei has come home to her. She dies a short time later after giving birth to a son, a renewal of life and purpose.

Characters

Pierre Bezukhov: Illegitimate son of Count Bezukhov, unsure of his rightful place in society.

Prince Andrei Bolkonsky: Russian army officer and husband of Princess Lisa.

General Kutuzov: Russian army officer and immediate superior to Andrei.

Princess Lisa: French wife of Andrei; she dies giving birth to their son.

Retired General-in-Chief Prince Nikolai Bolkonsky: Andrei's father; he exhorts him to be brave in battle.

Count Bezukhov: Critically ill father of Pierre.

Natasha Rostov: Carefree 13-year-old girl.

Helene Kurazin: Elegant but contemptuous bride of Pierre. She is rumored to have betrayed him.

Petya: Natasha's younger brother.

Napoleon: Emperor of France and commander of the Grand Army. He is fighting for personal glory and has conquered most of Europe.

Outline of Events

Note: During the opening scenes, words are shown in the subtitles very rapidly. Assure the students that they do not have to read every word to keep up with the plot of the story. Many of the words are listed in the vocabulary section of this guide.

1. With the threat of Napoleon's invasion of Russia, Russian elite meet at a salon, where the men are preoccupied with the inevitability of impending war. The wives are subdued, fearing the unknown.

2. Pierre and Andrei have a heart-to-heart talk, revealing their doubts and confusions to each other. Being the illegitimate son of Count Bezukhov, Pierre has no clearly defined goals for his life, having avoided marriage and military service. Knowing he is soon to become heir to the count's fortune, Pierre expresses concern about his life. Andrei, who has lived life as expected by his family, has a beautiful wife, Princess Lisa, who is pregnant with their first child, and a high position in the military. However, he tells Pierre he is bored with his marriage.

3. During their talk Andrei advises his friend, "Don't marry. Otherwise you will be making a cruel and irreparable mistake. Everything fine and noble in you will be wasted on trifles. I am trapped in this enchanted circle" (salons, gossip, balls, fripperies).

4. In spite of his indifference to his wife, Andrei assumes responsibility and makes plans for her to stay with his father and sister at Bald Hill, an estate outside St. Petersburg, during his absence. Princess Lisa, unhappy because of her husband's coldness, is reluctant to leave the family, friends, and high society that have been her life.

5. Lisa goes to live with Andrei's family at Bald Hill, and Andrei leaves for war. The battle scenes that ensue clearly show the technology and war tactics of the time. Battle scenes typical of the 18th and 19th centuries show pitched battles of advancing armies in regular rank and file.

6. While Andrei is at war, Pierre becomes the count after his bedridden father, Count Bezukhov, dies. The new Count Bezukhov, unsure of himself and awkward around women, becomes betrothed to a beautiful woman from Russia's high society. Events leading to the couple's engagement are embarrassingly clumsy and contrived.

7. In her new home, Princess Lisa has settled into a quiet life of sewing and making preparations for her baby. At the same time on the war front, General Kutuzov's Russian army has entered Austria. He is pessimistic about the Russo-Austrian prospects of beating the French on the eve of the

battle of Austerlitz. When Andrei asks the general, "What do you think about tomorrow?" he replies, "I think the battle will be lost."

8. After the Russian loss at Austerlitz, Andrei, wounded from the war, gains a new appreciation for his life.

9. Count Bezukhov's wife has been rumored to have been with Dolokov, a Russian soldier. Humiliated and angered, Count Bezukhov (Pierre) challenges Dolokov to a duel. Pierre wins, wounding but not killing his adversary. His wife, denying her relationship with Dolokov, expresses her contempt for Pierre by cruelly calling him names.

10. News from the war leads Andrei's family to believe he has been killed. When Andrei does return, he is greeted by a jubilant father and sister, while at the same time Princess Lisa is in the throes of a very painful and complicated childbirth. When Andrei goes to her bedside she looks at him through a mask of pain, unable to recognize he is there. She dies shortly after delivering their son.

11. Andrei visits the Rostov estate where he sees Natasha. Part I ends on a sad note, with Andrei in a state of depression.

Vocabulary

A lengthy list of words and phrases from the subtitles of this film is provided. From this list teachers can choose the words most appropriate for their classes. Words appear in chronological order so they may be introduced and reviewed as needed.

petitioning
minced words
enthroned
declaration of war
granting petitions
short shrift
renowned
emperor
maid of honor
hussar

confident
bequeathing
balance of power
inherit
Europe
grieve
powerful empire
deceived
reputedly
nicknamed

barbaric
specialist
intrigue
frightened
violence
affection
exile
sufferance
executions
ashamed
revolutions
Russian Army
ambassadors
commander-in-chief
wretched reception
tsar
revolution
mercenaries
deprived of
massacred
the pleasure of your company
great endeavor
political thermometer
solemn moment
ascertain
knapsacks
disposition
heroic endurance
court society
communicative
enlisting
nameday (birthday)
balance of power
banquet
diplomatic corps
campaign
egotists
idiocy
irreparable mistake
angel
trifles
laughing stock
soldier
superstition
diplomat
thinks he is dead
debauchery
strange coincidence
minced words

Before the Movie

1. Russia is on the brink of war with France. What would you do to prepare for the effects of war if your country were about to be invaded?

2. What are some ways people's lives are affected by war?

3. View the Hermitage by going to www.hermitagemuseum.org.

During the Movie

1. How would the Russian people's understanding of events on the battlefield during the early 1800s be different from our understanding today?

What technological advances make it possible to know events on faraway battlefields?

2. Pause the movie during a war scene. Briefly describe what you see.

After the Movie

1. Compare the lives of Andrei and Pierre. Which character did you like best and why?

2. Andrei was closer to Pierre than he was to his own wife or father. How can this bond be explained?

3. How do you think Andrei will cope with the loss of his wife? What do you think will be the focus of part II of *War and Peace*?

Language Arts Activities

Note: Many of the following activities contain actual words written by Leo Tolstoy. This provides opportunities for students to read and closely examine words and passages from one of the greatest writers of all time.

1. Andrei said, "Two misfortunes in life are remorse and illness. And the only good is the absence of these misfortunes." What is meant by this statement? Do you agree? Make a list of the characters in the film and their misfortunes. Have any of the characters avoided remorse and illness? Relate the statement to your life. (language arts standard 2)

2. Interpret the meaning of the following passage from the film, written by Tolstoy. Find passages that are the antithesis of each other. (language arts standard 1)

> Ever closer came that solemn moment
> for the sake of which so many trials and privation
> had been endured.
> Soldiers had been trained for 15 years,
> families and homes abandoned, peasants turned into army men.
> For the sake of that moment, thousands of men were living in the fields, on the roads, in the forests.

The familiar old life had gone.
To these men the road they trod
was not back to their former life
but to attack, to encirclement.
Houses were no longer family hearths,
but places of ambush.
Men were no longer brothers
but instruments of death and the victims of death.
One is afraid of the unknown
terrible, but glorious.

3. What is meant by the adage "Take time to smell the roses"? Discuss its meaning and relate the adage to your lives. The following passage conveys Andrei's thoughts as he lies injured, staring at the sky, in a semiconscious state. Relate Andrei's thoughts to the "take time to smell the roses" adage.

How quiet, how peaceful,
How solemn.
Different from the running, shouting, and firing.
How was it that I did not see the sky before?
And aren't I happy to have found it at last.
Yes, all is vanity,
All is delusion, except the infinite heavens.
There is nothing but the heavens.
And even they do not exist.
There is nothing but silence and stillness.
Glory to God.

Prior to the war Andrei confided to Pierre that life had no meaning; he was bored. Describe how you think Andrei's new awareness of life, based on his near-death experience, will affect his outlook on life. (language arts standards 1 and 2)

4. Andrei's wife died giving birth to a son in 1805. In 1823 his son will be 18 years old. Read the history of Russia after 1823 and determine what life will be like for Andrei's son as an adult. Write a brief description of your predictions about his life. (language arts standards 1, 2, and 5)

Social Studies Activities

1. Trace the route Napoleon took as he advanced to Austerlitz. Determine the distance from France to Austerlitz. (social studies standard III)

2. Discuss the following passage by Tolstoy, and relate it to events in the Middle East: "It is always the simplest ideas which lead to the greatest consequences. My idea, in its entirety, is that if vile people unite and constitute a force, then decent people are obliged to do likewise; just that." (social studies standard V)

3. Communications have changed greatly from the 1800s to now. Andrei's family believed for many weeks that he had been killed. Think of situations during battle and at home that required communications. List how people communicated in the early 1800s, and compare it with communications today. (social studies standards VIII and IX)

4. Napoleon defeated Austria. Russia and Austria united to resist Napoleon's advances in Europe. Compare life in Austria with life in Russia for both the noble and peasant classes. Relate the following song to both classes of people. (social studies standards IV and V)

> My home, my home, this is my new home.
> No more shall I see my own true home;
> No more will my sweetheart squeeze my hand.

Related Resources

Nonfiction

The Reign of Napoleon Bonaparte by Robert Asprey
St. Petersburg by Deborah Kent
Artillery of the Napoleonic Wars by Kevin Kiley
Tactics and the Experience of Battle in the Age of Napoleon by Rory Muir
Napoleon Bonaparte: A Life by Alan Schom
The Napoleonic Wars: Defeat of the Grand Army by Thomas Streissguth

Websites

Napoleon Guide, www.napoleonguide.com/leaders_kutusov.htm
World History at KMLA, *History of Warfare*, www.zum.de/whkmla/military/napwars/napinv.html

WAR AND PEACE, PART II

Grade Level: 9–12
Time: 95 minutes
Filmed: 1968 in color
Language: Russian and French
Genre: Epic history
Director: Sergei Bondarchuk
Rating: Not rated
Theme: Peace is simply a pleasant interlude between wars.
Interesting Fact: Tolstoy is considered to be one of the greatest writers of all time.
Setting: St. Petersburg, Russia, after the signing of the Treaty of Tilsit. Russia and France call an uneasy truce. Scenes of palaces, ballrooms, and the Russian countryside are prevalent.

Summary

Part I ended in the winter on a bleak and sad note: Andrei's wife died in childbirth, his father was ill, and the Russian army had been defeated by Napoleon's army at Austerlitz.

Part II begins in the spring when the protagonist, Andrei, is experiencing a rebirth. He has a renewed zest for life and a peaceful interlude from war to pursue life's pleasures.

In 1807, Napoleon and Alexander I of Russia sign the Treaty of Tilsit, which temporarily halts hostilities. Tolstoy provides an excellent description of Russian life during this time of peace. During this interlude of peace, Natasha is experiencing all that is wonderful about youth; she is exuberant, impulsive, and full of life. She falls wildly in love with Andrei during a dance at a ball for the cream of Russian aristocracy in 1810. Likewise, Andrei falls in love with the free-spirited Natasha. In concert with the frivolity and personal problems of the Russian aristocracy is the imminent attack on Russia by Napoleon's France.

This period of peace ends abruptly with Napoleon's invasion of Russia in 1812. Once again war is poised to destroy the lives of the people, including their hopes, dreams, and pledges of love.

Characters

Natasha Rostov: Beautiful, emotional, and impetuous young girl seeking love and a place in society.

Prince Andrei Bolkonsky: Officer in the Russian army who, following his wife's death, falls in love with Natasha.
Count Pierre Bezukhov: Illegitimate son of Count Bezukhov who has not found his place in Russian society. He is a close friend of Andrei and, though married, has feelings of love for Natasha.
Prince Anatole Kurazin: Married suitor of Natasha.
Sonya: Natasha's best friend.
Petya: Natasha's younger brother.

Outline of Events

1. After the signing of the Treaty of Tilsit in 1807, Russia is at peace. The Russian aristocracy is shown once again socializing and dancing in an opulent ballroom, while at the same time, Napoleon is planning the invasion of Russia.

2. Natasha attends the ball and is nervously standing next to her mother, wondering whether anyone will ask her to dance. Men and women are shown dancing the equivalent of modern-day line dancing. Andrei approaches Natasha and asks her to dance. They dance majestically as though in a fairy tale; Natasha and Andrei, oblivious to all but the music and each other, fall in love.

3. Dual scenes show Andrei confiding his feelings about Natasha to his friend Pierre, while at the same time Natasha confides her love of Andrei to her mother. Andrei tells Pierre, "The whole world is split into two for me; with her is happiness, hope, light. The other half without her is all gloom and darkness."

4. Natasha, expecting to hear from Andrei after the dance, does not hear from him for three weeks, leaving her uncertain about his love. She goes through long periods of self-doubt, telling herself she doesn't need anyone, that she is fine alone. Andrei returns to a relieved and overjoyed Natasha and proposes marriage. Natasha's childlike eagerness and immediate acceptance adversely affect Andrei. The shift in his attitude from passionate love to the love one feels for a child is best expressed in Tolstoy's words: "He could not find in his heart his former love for her. It had suddenly changed from the poetic charm of desire to pity for her feminine

and childlike fragility and to fear at her devotion and trustfulness." (It's too easy.) "Though not so romantic and poetic as before the new sentiment was deeper and stronger."

5. Though the romance has diminished, Andrei's love for Natasha has grown deeper. Andrei tells her that they must wait a year before announcing their engagement. Natasha, unaware of the change in Andrei's love for her, reluctantly accepts Andrei's plan. Andrei leaves to defend his country against Napoleon's invasion, and Natasha resumes her life.

6. While on a foxhunt with her uncle and brother, Natasha meets a "scoundrel of a man," Prince Anatole. Though he is married, he tells her that without her he will die. While at the hunting lodge, Natasha impresses everyone with her beautiful dancing. Her uncle observes that dancing is in the blood of every man and woman in Russia.

7. Prince Anatole and his friend Dolokov are plotting to kidnap Natasha, while Petya and Sonya are plotting to save her from Anatole. Natasha, angry with Petya and Sonya for interfering, angrily states that she loves Anatole. However, after the foiled plot, Anatole leaves Natasha. When Andrei comes home and learns about her liaison with Anatole, he leaves her as well. Shamed and alone, Natasha goes to Pierre, telling him she has lost everything.

8. Pierre, unhappily married to a woman who scorns and demeans him, has fallen in love with Natasha. Being honorable and loyal, he keeps his love to himself. However, he wishes he were a better man, more clever and handsome and free, so he could win the love of Natasha.

9. The Russian Orthodox Church is shown actively supporting the Russian army. There is great excitement and cheering in the streets. One intensely poignant scene shows fresh, young Russian troops being cheered as they march off to war past exhausted, injured troops returning from the war.

10. The French army enters Russia. People are shown celebrating both war and peace with equal vigor. This conundrum is expressed by Tolstoy: "On the 12th of June, 1812, the Forces of Western Europe crossed the Frontiers of Russia and war began. In other words, an event took place that was contrary to all human reason and human nature."

Vocabulary

A lengthy list of words and phrases from the subtitles of this film is provided. From this list teachers can choose the words most appropriate for their classes. Words appear in chronological order so they may be introduced and reviewed as needed.

intimacy
depressed
virtuous
comical
astonishing
overcoat
emperor
Egyptians
Diplomatic Corps
immortal
treasure
eternity
impossible
murmurs
betrothed
elope
soldiers
invalid
refuge
abroad
balalaika
comrades
renowned
disgraced
inimitable
scoundrel
cockerel
ignoble
Madagascar
comet
melancholy
frontier
regiment

Before the Movie

1. Recall the ending of Part I. What do you think Andrei will do with his life?

2. Read about the Treaty of Tilsit. How long did it last? What effect did it have on the invasion of Russia?

3. Compare the lifestyles of Pierre and Andrei. How are they different, and how are they alike?

4. What characters do you like best in the film? Describe the reasons for your choices.

During the Movie

1. What caused Andrei's love for Natasha to change? Think about a time when your feelings for a person have changed.

2. Compare the types of entertainment in Russian high society with entertainment today.

After the Movie

1. Though most of the focus in this film was on peace, the final scenes showed Russian soldiers being cheered as they went off to war. What role did religion play in the war?

2. What do you think will happen to Andrei? Do you think he will marry Natasha?

3. What changes do you think will occur in Russian society after the war? Will the people continue to have the same lavish soirées and balls?

4. What are your impressions of the social life of the aristocratic Russians? Compare your impressions with your own social experiences. Which do you prefer and why?

Language Arts Activities

Note: Two of the following activities contain actual words written by Leo Tolstoy. This provides opportunities for students to read and closely examine words and passages from one of the greatest writers of all time.

1. Individually or in small groups, research Russian composers who lived before 1812. Choose a Russian composer and write a description. Include ideas on ways society in the late 1700s influenced the composers' style of music. Present your information to the class, supported by a sample of the music. (language arts standards 1, 4, and 7)

2. Reenact scenes from the film, paying attention to the feelings, attitudes, and actions of individual characters. For example, Natasha can be portrayed not only as a young girl in love but also as someone who, at this

point, is more concerned about her own affairs than the war. (language arts standards 3 and 4)

3. Write a passage about how each of the main characters view life during the time of peace and normalcy described in the film: (language arts standards 2 and 6)

> Life meanwhile, that is people's real lives with their real concerns of health and illnesses, work and relaxation, their interests in ideas, science, poetry, music, love, friendship, hatred, passion, life meanwhile continued as usual. Independent and regardless of political alliance or enmity with Napoleon Bonaparte.

4. Read Tolstoy's words regarding Andrei's feelings for Natasha and choose one of the activities below. (language arts standards 2 and 6)

"He could not find in his heart his former love for her. It had suddenly changed from the poetic charm of desire to pity for her feminine and childlike fragility."

a. Write a love letter to Natasha explaining your changed feelings toward her.
b. Write a love letter to Andrei expressing your feelings of concern over having to wait a year before announcing your engagement.

Social Studies Activities

1. Read about the Treaty of Tilsit. What effect did it have on all of Europe? What caused the end of the treaty, and how did it affect Russia? (social studies standards II and V)

2. The Treaty of Tilsit lasted five years, from 1807 to 1812. During this time Russia was experiencing a period of peace. What were the activities and interests of the women during this respite between battles? What were the activities and interests of the men? Compare and contrast the activities and interests of the men and women. (social studies standard IV)

3. Read about Napoleon's advance on Russia. Where were his troops located during the period of peace enforced by the Treaty of Tilsit? What

parts of Russia were the intermediate targets of Napoleon's advance to Moscow? (social studies standard III)

4. Look at a map of Russia. Determine how Napoleon arranged to get food and supplies to his troops. How far is it from Paris to Moscow? (social studies standard III)

Related Resources

Nonfiction

The Reign of Napoleon Bonaparte by Robert Asprey
St. Petersburg by Deborah Kent
Artillery of the Napoleonic Wars by Kevin Kiley
Tactics and the Experience of Battle in the Age of Napoleon by Rory Muir
Napoleon Bonaparte: A Life by Alan Schom
The Napoleonic Wars: Defeat of the Grand Army by Thomas Streissguth

Music

Beethoven's Symphony no. 5

Websites

Napoleon Guide, www.napoleonguide.com/leaders_kutusov.htm
World History at KMLA, *History of Warfare*, www.zum.de/whkmla/military/napwars/napinv.html

WAR AND PEACE, PART III

Grade Level: 9–12
Time: 77 minutes
Filmed: 1968 in color
Language: Russian and French
Genre: Epic history
Director: Sergei Bondarchu
Rating: Not rated (blurred nude male backsides in bathing scenes)
Theme: War is accompanied by hardship, failed dreams, and death, rarely by glory.

Interesting Fact: Tolstoy said, "To write a good book one must love its basic fundamental ideas. In *War and Peace* I loved the people's emotions arising from the War of 1812."
Setting: St. Petersburg, Russia, and the battlefield of Borodino in 1812 during Napoleon's march to Moscow.

Summary

Part II ended with Russia on the brink of war. The period of peace from 1807 to 1812 was shattered by Napoleon's invasion of Russia.

Part III begins with the French army, commanded by Napoleon, marching east into western Russia, while at the same time officers of the Russian army and the social elite are dancing and socializing at a magnificent ball in St. Petersburg. The contrast between the colorful and elegant clothes, lively dances, and blissful ignorance of the Russian people's plight and Napoleon's ceaseless march to the east is striking.

As word of Napoleon's impending invasion spreads among the people, preadolescent boys beg their parents to let them fight to protect their fatherland. Priests in Russian Orthodox churches offer prayers. Sermons and pronouncements against the French have a similar theme: "Confront and put to shame them that devise evil against us and may the mighty angel chastise and defeat them. Smite our enemies and be swift to vanquish them."

Churchmen and the general citizenry line the streets to cheer the boys and men going off to war. Russian nobility meet to discuss politics. Scenes of Russian villages being burned by the French and of frightened villagers fleeing for their lives show the brutal realities of war. As fresh, enthusiastic Russian soldiers march off to war, they pass the wounded and weary soldiers returning from the front.

Priests, wearing colorful robes and carrying icons and flags, join the troops on the battlefield. This colorful pageantry combined with scenes of 100,000 people genuflecting on the eve of the Battle of Borodino shows the importance of the church in the lives of the Russian people.

The Battle of Borodino was the turning point in the War of 1812. Both sides were considerably weakened because of enormous casualties. Napoleon and the Russian commander, Kutuzov, have difficult choices to make concerning the final battle for Moscow.

Characters

Prince Andrei Bolkonsky: Regimental commander whose regiment is present at the Battle of Borodino but held in reserve.
Retired General-in-Chief Prince Nikolai Bolkonsky: Andrei's father, who dies brokenhearted, believing his beloved Russia will soon be lost to Napoleon.
General Barclay de Tolly: Commanding general of the Russian army. He loses his command to Kutuzov because of his retreat from Vitebsk.
General Kutuzov: Aging commanding general of the Russian army who replaces Barclay. He once again becomes Andrei's immediate superior and leads his army in a gallant battle against Napoleon's Grand Army at Borodino.
Napoleon: Emperor of France and commander of the Grand Army. He is fighting for personal glory and has conquered most of Europe.
Count Pierre Bezukhov: A close friend of Andrei. Still trying to find a way to serve his country, Pierre joins the soldiers on the battlefield, looking out of place in his off-white gentleman's suit.
Natasha Rostov: Andrei's fiancée. She seeks Pierre's counsel.
Prince Anatole Kurazin: A rival for Natasha's affections, he meets up with Andrei in a hospital in Moscow.

Outline of Events

Prologue:

> On June 12, 1812, the French entered Vitebsk, on their way to Moscow. They are within four days of reaching Smolensk. Barclay retreated leaving Vitebsk to Napoleon. Because of this retreat, he lost his command to Kutuzov. Kutuzov, in spite of his advanced age, resumed command and has become the field marshal.

1. The Russian high society, including military officers, are together at a ball while Napoleon's army is advancing east into western Russia. Some socially elite officials make fun of Andrei's superior, General Kutuzov, saying he is blind and too old to be of any use.

2. Meanwhile, the Russian army is suffering major defeats from the French. Soldiers going to war make fun of Pierre and his fancy clothes as

they pass him by. Participation in the war is glorified by church services and large cheering crowds. Preadolescent boys beg their parents to let them join the army. The celebratory mood of the people in St. Petersburg, yet unaffected by the war, is countered by scenes of villages being burned by the French and people fleeing for their lives.

3. Andrei's father, retired General Bolkonsky, is at home. His thoughts are addled, believing the theater of war is in Poland. He is worried but too old to come to the aid of his country, a sad end to a brilliant military career. He dies brokenhearted, thinking his beloved Russia is destroyed.

4. Andrei, awaiting the Battle of Borodino, sends the following letter home: "Our armies are fighting as never before. The fate of the army and of the fatherland is in the hands of a good minister, but Barclay is a bad commander. He is sluggish. The whole army detests him."

5. Back in St. Petersburg, Pierre hears Natasha sing and falls deeper in love. Natasha, though still in love with Andrei, tells Pierre that he is very important to her.

6. While surveying the troops, new Field Marshal Kutuzov sees Andrei and tries to recruit him to be a member of his staff. Andrei chooses to remain with his regiment. Kutuzov praises Andrei for his honor, saying there are too many advisors and not enough fighting men.

7. The desire to make sacrifices and to be useful draws Pierre inexorably toward the imminent battle. He goes to the battlefield dressed in a fancy suit. At the front, he becomes a curiosity and a spectator. Once again Pierre does not fit in, vacillating between being a gentleman and wanting to serve in a very bloody and messy war.

8. A stunning scene shows the deep religious connection of the Russian Orthodox Church to the Russian army. Dressed in magnificent robes, clergy carrying banners and icons of Mary and Jesus march with the soldiers. With patriotic and religious fervor, the soldiers make peace with God before engaging in the largest battle of the war.

9. On the eve of the Battle of Borodino, Andrei predicts his own death. Pierre comes to visit him. Andre tells Pierre, "War is not a sport, but the

vilest thing in life." Andrei and Pierre part, each believing they will not see each other again.

10. During the Battle of Borodino a mud-splattered Pierre watches from different command posts. Andrei's unit is held in reserve and does not see action. As Andrei walks away from his unit, a live cannonball lands close to him. Events unfold in slow motion, with Andrei thinking, "I don't want to die. I love life." The cannonball explodes, gravely injuring him.

11. Upon awakening in the hospital, Andrei sees Prince Anatole, the man Andrei believes stole his beloved Natasha. They exchange painful looks, grieving for themselves and their country.

12. Though technically a French victory, the Russians, despite losing more than 40% of their troops, claim a strategic victory at the Battle of Borodino. Napoleon, surveying the ruins of his army, is dismayed at the high number of losses the Grand Army suffered.

Vocabulary

A lengthy list of words and phrases from the subtitles of this film is provided. From this list teachers can choose the words most appropriate for their classes. Words appear in chronological order so they may be introduced and reviewed as needed.

emperor
advisor
general
campaign
decrepit
peasants
blind man's bluff
Moscow
opinion
casualties
theatre (theater) of war
sacrifices
Poland
hardship
satisfactory
inexorably
oppressive
imminent
destroyed
enemy
St. George's Cross
ordeal
generous
guards have been posted

Before the Movie

1. Do you think churches should support military troops? Look for the connections between the Russian Orthodox Church and the Russian army as you view the film.

2. What do you think Napoleon is doing during the time of peace brought about by the Treaty of Tilsit?

During the Movie

1. Why do you think young boys are so eager to join the Russian army?

2. Which character or organization in the film do you think is most admirable and why?

After the Movie

1. Describe your feelings after seeing the returning haggard Russian troops pass freshly recruited troops going off to war.

2. What were some of the horrors of war experienced by the Russian people?

3. On a map, find the area of Russia that was the site of the Battle of Borodino. Why was it such a strategic area?

4. Russia claimed a strategic victory after the Battle of Borodino. What does this mean?

Language Arts Activities

To set the mood, play Tchaikovsky's *1812 Overture* during the activities.

1. Some of the Russian soldiers insulted Generals Kutuzov and Barclay. Research facts about each general. Write a brief description that captures the characteristics of the generals. Do your best to make the generals come to life for your audience. (language arts standards 1, 6, and 7)

2. Using imagery to guide your words, write a description of what it would have been like to live in a Russian village in the path of the advancing French army. (language arts standard 6)

3. As people fled their homes and villages, they took all they could carry with them and burned the rest. Describe being an occupant of the village from either the point of view of a villager or an exhausted and hungry French soldier. (language arts standard 6)

Social Studies Activities

1. Vitebsk is said to be a four-day march from Smolensk. Look at a map and determine how many miles or kilometers separate the villages. How did people communicate with each other in 1812? (social studies standards III and VII)

2. Draw a map showing Napoleon's march through Russia. Label the cities where battles took place including Vitebsk, Smolensk, and Borodino. Note the distance from these battles to Moscow. Which major rivers did the French have to cross? (social studies standard III)

3. The battles of Vitebsk, Smolensk, and Borodino were fought in the mid to late summer. Research the climate of these Russian cities. What effect did the weather have on the troops of the French and Russian armies? Which army was most likely to be adversely affected by the weather? Why? (social studies standard III)

Resources

Nonfiction

The Reign of Napoleon Bonaparte by Robert Asprey
1812: Napoleon's Invasion of Russia by Paul Britten Austin
St. Petersburg by Deborah Kent
Artillery of the Napoleonic Wars by Kevin Kiley
Tactics and the Experience of Battle in the Age of Napoleon by Rory Muir
Napoleon Bonaparte: A Life by Alan Schom
The Napoleonic Wars: Defeat of the Grand Army by Thomas Streissguth

Music

Tchaikovsky's *1812 Overture*

Websites

Napoleon Guide, www.napoleonguide.com/leaders_kutusov.htm
World History at KMLA, *History of Warfare*, www.zum.de/whkmla/military/napwars/napinv.html

WAR AND PEACE, PART IV

Grade Level: 9–12
Time: 93 minutes
Filmed: 1968 in color
Language: Russian and French
Genre: Epic history
Director: Sergei Bondarchuk
Rating: Not rated
Theme: In love and war, patience is a virtue.
Interesting Fact: Tolstoy agonized about the meaning of life. His preoccupation with the meaning of life is woven throughout the four parts of *War and Peace*.
Setting: September 1 to October 19, 1812, in Moscow before and after the city is pillaged and burned, followed by the wintry retreat of Napoleon's army across western Russia.

Summary

Part III ended with Napoleon's push to the Russian capital, Moscow. Both the French and Russian troops had suffered tremendous losses in the Battle of Borodino.

Part IV begins with Kutuzov's understanding that the salvation of Russia depends on having a strong army. Realizing he can't defeat Napoleon without decimating his own army, Kutuzov gives the order to leave Moscow, hoping to strand Napoleon without any means of providing for his troops. Napoleon's supply lines have been stretched thin, and his troops, now thousands of miles from France, will soon have little food or protection from the freezing temperatures.

Sitting on his horse on a hill, Napoleon looks down on his prize, Moscow, the Russian capital. He proclaims, "Here it is. . . . Holy capital lying at my feet, it awaits its fate." However, by the time Napoleon and his men enter Moscow, it is eerily quiet. Flocks of birds are the only obvious signs of life. Pierre, planning to fight for his country by killing

Napoleon, is among the few people remaining. Unknown to Napoleon, Moscow has been stripped by fleeing Muscovites in an attempt to starve and freeze his army. History is unclear whether it was the Russians or the French who burned Moscow, or perhaps a combination of both. With all the buildings aflame, Napoleon concentrates his efforts on saving the Kremlin, his new headquarters.

During the French occupation of Moscow, the Russian army menaces Napoleon. With dwindling supplies, he is forced to retreat as winter comes. Kutuzov pursues what is left of Napoleon's Grand Army. Both Kutuzov and Napoleon give farewell addresses to their troops. Kutuzov thanks his troops, saying victory is complete. Napoleon gives a lengthy speech during his army's retreat from Moscow. Men in the proudly hailed Grand Army, who had traveled all the way from France, must now retrace their steps, this time in the frigid conditions of winter. The juxtaposition between the spirited words of Napoleon's farewell address and his dispirited troops is striking. As Napoleon praises his troops, they are dropping from cold, hunger, and exhaustion. In spite of his artful rhetoric, Napoleon's once mighty army is demoralized and decimated.

Characters

Napoleon: Emperor of France and leader of the Grand Army. Fighting for personal glory, he eagerly anticipates the riches of Moscow.

General Kutuzov: Aging commanding general of the Russian army. He issues a controversial order to retreat from Moscow.

Prince Andrei Bolkonsky: Regimental commander who lies mortally wounded in a hospital in Moscow.

Count Pierre Bezukhov: A close friend of Andrei. He has found satisfaction by helping the Russian people as they evacuate the capital. He is taken as a prisoner of war.

Natasha Rostov: Andrei's fiancée; she comforts Andrei as he lies dying and reassures him of her love. She also has deep feelings for Pierre.

Petya: Natasha's younger brother. He is killed in battle.

Outline of Events

1. After consulting his aides, Kutuzov makes the excruciatingly difficult decision to retreat from Moscow to preserve the Russian army. His

thoughts are anguished as he asks himself, "Can I really have allowed Napoleon to reach Moscow?"

2. Napoleon is sitting on a hilltop outside of Moscow. He is anticipating occupying the Russian capital with all its riches. Meanwhile, Russian citizens are fleeing their homes. They donate their carts, needed to carry their possessions, to the soldiers transporting the wounded. Pierre, who has elected to remain in Moscow, sees Natasha among the evacuees. They speak briefly and say good-bye.

3. Napoleon's aides notify him that Moscow is almost empty; 250,000 people have fled. Flocks of pigeons precede Napoleon on his way to the Kremlin.

4. Pierre remains in his mansion in Moscow, with plans to kill Napoleon. French soldiers, led by Captain Ramballe, enter his mansion. A drunken servant fires his gun at the French captain, and Pierre saves the captain's life. Speaking French, Pierre and Captain Ramballe strike up a friendship.

5. Napoleon is in awe, surrounded by riches and gold. He is intrigued by the lavish buildings with the Russian onion domes. While Napoleon is admiring the city, it begins to burn. All of Moscow seems to be on fire; a dreadful glow is seen throughout the city. During this time Pierre saves a young child. This heroic act seems to awaken his purpose for living. During the time his best friend Andrei is dying, Pierre is gaining a new spirit for living. Instead of quietly observing life from the sidelines, he now asserts himself. When he sees a French soldier stealing another man's boots, he rushes to the man's aid.

6. Life in St. Petersburg is dramatically different from life in Moscow. People continue their daily lives without interruption. During this time, Pierre's wife, Helene, dies.

7. Accused of being a Russian spy, Pierre is imprisoned with his fellow Russian citizens. He is marched with the other prisoners, men and boys, to the execution site, where he watches them be executed. Pierre escapes execution but is haunted by what he has witnessed. Scenes flash through his mind. He wonders whether others are as sickened as he is.

8. Andrei, mortally wounded during the Battle of Borodino, is visited by Natasha. Upon seeing her he says, "What happiness." Natasha asks Andrei for forgiveness. They both profess their love for one another. Natasha stays by his bedside while Maria, Andrei's sister, and Nikolai, his son, come to say good-bye. Andrei once again sees the same scenes of clouds and sky that he saw when he lay wounded on the battlefield at Austerlitz.

9. With few supplies and freezing winter temperatures, the French approach General Kutuzov and ask for a settlement. He refuses, declaring that he wants to drive the invaders from Russia's sacred land. Napoleon is desperately trying to negotiate a settlement but receives no answer from Tsar Alexander I. Kutuzov plans to attack Napoleon during his retreat from Moscow.

10. The French have taken the Russian prisoners on their retreat. Pierre is among them. The French are ordered to shoot any prisoner who falls behind. The Russians also take prisoners. Because of the brutal conditions, the French and the Russians find a strange camaraderie. They sing French songs and share food and drink. One Russian soldier observes, "They are men just like us."

11. Natasha's younger brother, Petya, a Russian soldier, is killed during battle.

12. Napoleon gives his last address to his troops during their retreat from France. Initially, the French soldiers march in ranks in close-order drill, but their formations become more and more ragged as Napoleon continues his farewell speech to his troops:

> Soldiers! I have kept my promise to you. You have seen your Emperor sharing your dangers and hardships. I want you to see him surrounded by the grandeur and splendor which is due to the sovereign of the greatest people in the world. Soldiers! The Austrian and Italian armies once sullied our provinces; they claimed they would destroy my crown; that they now, thanks to you, are scattered, defeated, and destroyed is proof of my maxim. God gave me the crown, woe to him who touches it. Soldiers! When I promised peace to the French people, I spoke for you. I know your worth. You are the same men who can guard the Rhine, Holland, Italy, and dictated peace at Vienna. Soldiers! All of you want to return to France in honor. We

> can only return beneath triumphal arches. Soldiers! The battle you have longed for is at hand. Victory depends on you; it is essential to all our needs. It will ensure comfortable quarters and a quick return to our homeland. Acquit yourselves as at Austerlitz, Friedland, Vitebsk, and Smolensk. Posterity will proudly recall your achievements this day. Of each of you it may be said, "He fought at the gates of Moscow."

13. At the end of his speech, Napoleon is talking to corpses and shells of men. The French army is decimated by the Russian winter. The surviving French army is reduced to eating horseflesh to stay alive.

14. The Russians have regrouped. Captain Ramballe is now a prisoner of the Russians. There is great singing and cheering. The rebuilding of Moscow has begun. Pierre, now free, is remembering young Natasha. He is eager to return to St. Petersburg to be with her.

Vocabulary

A lengthy list of words and phrases from the subtitles of this film is provided. From this list teachers can choose the words most appropriate for their classes. Words appear in chronological order so they may be introduced and reviewed as needed.

military
perish
salvation of Russia
icons
advantage
provisions
battle
incendiary
opinion
sovereign
sacred capital
tranquil
horrified
luxurious
thousands
bishop
brunt
insolent
authority
brazen
realm
horseflesh
humble
issued an order
unanimously
wounded
condemned
discharged

executing
pistol
yearnings
peasant
fret
betrothed
injustice
confusing
regiment
crumbling
spiritual struggle
majestic city
anxious
deputation
eternal
clemency
posterity
dreadful glow
instigation
mortally wounded
grandeur
incognito
splendor

Before the Movie

1. Review Napoleon's goal of empire building. Read about countries under his control in 1812.

2. What difficulties might Napoleon's army encounter during their final push into Russia's capital?

During the Movie

1. What are some of the decisions Kutuzov and Napoleon made during the course of the siege of Moscow? Who do you think made the best decisions for his army?

2. Do you agree or disagree with Kutuzov's decision to pull out of Moscow, leaving it to Napoleon?

After the Movie

1. Pause or turn off the movie during the end of Napoleon's farewell address to his troops. Discuss the images that are shown.

2. How do you think Pierre's newly found purpose in life will affect his future actions?

Language Arts Activities

To set the mood, play Tchaikovsky's *1812 Overture* during the activities.

1. Napoleon is known to have engaged in war for his own glory. Read Napoleon's farewell speech (Outline of Events, number 12, page 217). What evidence do you see of Napoleon's egocentricism? Given the state of his troops while he was speaking, what do you think of the content of the speech itself? Do you think Napoleon was delusional? (language arts standards 3 and 6)

2. Using a divided piece of paper write Napoleon's farewell speech to his troops (Outline of Events, number 12, page 217) on one side. On the other side, rewrite Napoleon's speech with a message you would give the soldiers. (language arts standards 2, 3, 4, and 6)

3. Tolstoy said, "To write a good book one must love its basic fundamental ideas." Apply his thinking to any writing project. Think about your own writing. Why is it important to love the fundamental ideas of what you are writing? When do you find writing the easiest and most rewarding? (language arts standard 5)

4. Working individually or in small groups, determine the most significant historical facts and concepts you learned while viewing this film. Prepare a report to share with others. (language arts standards 5 and 11)

5. Would you have liked to have lived in Russia during the time of 1805–1812? Why or why not? What part of Russia would you choose? Explain your choice. (language arts standard 12)

6. Listen critically to Tchaikovsky's *1812 Overture*. In his work you can hear themes from Russian folk songs, along with cannon fire. Draw a picture that depicts Russian life presented through music. (language arts standard 7)

7. Consider the following quote made by a French officer: "Napoleon was the greatest man of all time past and future." Read about Napoleon and determine whether you agree or disagree with the officer's statement. (language arts standards 1 and 2)

Social Studies Activities

1. Create a map of the Napoleonic Empire in 1812. (social studies standard III)

2. Looking at a topographical map of the Napoleonic Empire, 1805–1815, list the difficulties Napoleon faced getting supplies to his troops. Assume the role of a high-ranking French supply officer. Considering landforms and climate, determine routes you would use to get supplies to the troops. (social studies standard III)

3. Make a timeline of Napoleon's actions and determine how and when the downfall of Napoleon began. (social studies standard II)

4. Napoleon's ambitions were power and glory. Assume the role of Napoleon, and write a journal of events about one of your military campaigns. Include information from your topographical map about the geography as well as your military goals and ambitions. (social studies standards III and IV)

5. Napoleon met defeat in Russia. Even though he had a massive army, his invasion was doomed. What factors would account for Napoleon's defeat? Assume the role of a French soldier and write a letter home describing the conditions of your life and the battle with the Russians. Include information about the weapons used by you and the enemy. (social studies standards IV and VI)

6. *War and Peace* is considered to be an antiwar commentary. Think critically of the film's depiction of the Napoleonic Wars and determine how it may or may not have glorified war. (social studies standard II)

7. How was Russian history repeated from 1941 to 1945 by another western European power? (social studies standard II)

Related Resources

Nonfiction

The Reign of Napoleon Bonaparte by Robert Asprey
1812: The Great Retreat: Told by Survivors by Paul Britten Austin

With Napoleon in Russia: The Illustrated Memoirs of Faber Du Faur, 1812 by Christian Wilhelm von Faber Du Faur, translated by Jonathan North
1812: Through Fire and Ice With Napoleon: A French Officer's Memoir of the Campaign by Eugene Labaume
Tactics and the Experience of Battle in the Age of Napoleon by Rory Muir
Napoleon Bonaparte: A Life by Alan Schom
The Napoleonic Wars: Defeat of the Grand Army by Thomas Streissguth
Imperial Legend: The Mysterious Disappearance of Tsar Alexander I by Alexis S. Troubetzkoy
The Diary of a Napoleonic Foot Soldier by Jakob Walter
Moscow 1812: Napoleon's Fatal March by Adam Zamoyski

Music

Tchaikovsky's *1812 Overture*

Game

Strategy (Milton Bradley)

Websites

Napoleon Guide, www.napoleonguide.com/leaders_kutusov.htm
World History at KMLA, *History of Warfare*, www.zum.de/whkmla/military/napwars/napinv.html

WUTHERING HEIGHTS

Grade Level: 9–12
Time: 91 minutes
Filmed: 1954 in black and white
Language: Spanish
Genre: Gothic tale
Director: Luis Buñuel
Rating: Not rated
Theme: Revenge is destruction with an excuse.
Interesting Facts: Luis Buñuel had to make do with a cast that had previously been hired for another movie. Through his directing, the actors

and actresses beautifully portray the characters in Buñuel's Mexican adaptation of the English classic by Emily Brontë.

Wuthering Heights is the best-selling book in the United Kingdom.

Setting: Mexico's High Chaparral in the early 1800s. Scenes include the home of Eduardo and Catalina, the nearby home of Ricardo, and the surrounding countryside of dry scrub brush and trees.

Summary

The following passage is from the opening scene of the film:

> This picture is based on *Wuthering Heights*, the immortal words of Emily Brontë, written more than a hundred years ago.
>
> Its characters are at the mercy of their instincts and passions.
>
> They are unique beings for whom the so-called social conventions do not exist.
>
> Alejandro's love for Catalina is a fierce and inhuman feeling that can only be fulfilled through death.
>
> More importantly, this picture tries to remain true to the spirit of Emily Brontë's novel.

This is a gothic tale illuminating the dark side of a dysfunctional family. It is the story of love twisted by fanaticism, where blind fury and passion collide with decency and reason. Catalina, comfortably married to Eduardo, sees again her one true love, Alejandro. Their flaming passion makes it impossible for them to ignore their feelings for one another. Catalina, pregnant by her husband, is in frail health. In spite of her loyalties to Eduardo, she is inevitably drawn to Alejandro, having neither the will nor the strength to resist his impassioned demands.

When Catalina initially rejects Alejandro's advances, he marries Eduardo's sister, Isabel, for revenge. Isabel, falling in love with the handsome, dark suitor, learns too late about his harsh and abusive ways. She realizes that his love will always be for Catalina.

Because Alejandro would rather die than lose Catalina, he is a formidable foe, leaving Eduardo helpless to keep the woman he loves. Death becomes the only way for Catalina and Alejandro to be together in love.

Characters

Eduardo: Catalina's wealthy husband.
Catalina: Married to one man and passionately in love with another.
Alejandro: Deranged by an impossible love for Catalina. He marries her sister-in-law for revenge.
Isabel: Eduardo's loyal sister. She falls in love with Alejandro.
Ricardo: Catalina's drunken, abusive brother.
Jorito: Ricardo's son. He receives the brunt of Ricardo's abusive behavior.
Maria: Loyal servant to Eduardo and Catalina.
Old man: Tries to exorcise evil from Ricardo's house through prayerful rituals.

Outline of Events

1. A cool exchange between Eduardo and Catalina introduces their strained relationship. Eduardo deeply loves his wife and longs to have her return his love.

2. Alejandro arrives at Eduardo and Catalina's house and forcibly enters despite the efforts of the servant, Maria, to stop him. Alejandro shows the depths of his demented soul when he fiercely professes his undying love for Catalina. Upon seeing Alejandro, Eduardo orders him out of the house. Shaken by what he saw, Eduardo professes his love to Catalina and is rebuffed. She later admits that she does love him, but in a different way from how she loves Alejandro.

3. Isabel, seeing Alejandro, falls madly in love with him and seeks to be with Catalina and Alejandro at every opportunity. Catalina tells Alejandro that though she will always love him, even in death, she can't leave Eduardo because she is carrying his baby. In anger and to spite Catalina, Alejandro marries Isabel. During their short marriage he is abusive to Isabel, telling Catalina that he hates Isabel because she has Eduardo's eyes.

4. Catalina is critically ill before the imminent birth of her baby. Alejandro once again forces himself into Eduardo's home and passionately embraces Catalina. Eduardo encounters the couple and orders Alejandro to leave. Catalina collapses and dies after giving birth to her baby.

5. Ricardo, Catalina's brother, a drunk and compulsive gambler, owes money and his house to Alejandro. Ricardo tries to convince Isabel to help him kill Alejandro. When Alejandro arrives home, she is to open the door and he will shoot him. Isabel is unable to be a party to her husband's death and warns Alejandro to leave. Alejandro, knowing that Catalina has died, runs to her cemetery plot. Seeing that her body has not been moved to its final resting place, a bereaved and crazed Alejandro returns to Eduardo's home, opens the casket, kisses Catalina, and then is shot by Ricardo. Alejandro tumbles into the casket on top of Catalina's body.

6. At last Alejandro's wish to be with Catalina is fulfilled as he joins her, fatally wounded, in her casket.

Vocabulary

A lengthy list of words and phrases from the subtitles of this film is provided. From this list teachers can choose the words most appropriate for their classes. Words appear in chronological order so they may be introduced and reviewed as needed.

buzzards
threatened
ridiculous
condemned
dissection
furious
butterflies
mortgage
liberty
neighbor
incorrigible
tenderness
mistress
repulsive worm
servant
impartial
act accordingly
punishment

fatigue
indigestion
savage
quarrels
permission
very critical
lost a fortune gambling
writhe
tribulations
reproach
salvation
regained consciousness
jealous
abyss
ride five leagues
infidels
alright (all right)
consultation

nauseate
disintegrated
lantern
betray
revenge

Before the Movie

1. What is the difference between loyalty and love? Which one do you think is stronger?

2. How do you think fanatical love affects not only the lovers but the people around them?

During the Movie

1. How does the black and white background set the mood for the story?

2. Do you think Catalina should leave Eduardo for Alejandro? Why or why not?

After the Movie

1. Do you believe in a one true love? Why or why not?

2. What role did revenge play in the story?

3. What do you think will happen to Eduardo and his newborn baby?

Language Arts Activities

1. The words from the subtitles in this film conjure up thoughts of evil and depravity. Make a list of words from the film that you think added to the film's message and story. (language arts standard 1)

2. Make a list of the main characters, and describe their dominant personality traits. Keeping the personalities of the characters intact, rewrite the ending of the story. (language arts standards 5 and 6)

3. Read passages from the English version of *Wuthering Heights*. Compare Mexican and English versions of the characters, problems, and resolutions. (language arts standard 3)

4. *Romeo and Juliet* also told the story of two lovers destined to die. Compare the similarities and differences between both classics. (language arts standard 2)

Social Studies Activities

1. Make a list of the characters. Connect the history of each character to each of the other characters. A flowchart would be helpful to organize this information. Describe ways the characters' lives have changed over time. (social studies standards II and IV)

2. Emily Brontë's novel W*uthering Heights* was set on the moors of England. Luis Buñuel chose the desolate high plains of Mexico for the setting of his film. Research both geographical areas, and compare their similarities and differences. Describe how the setting affects the story. (social studies standard IV)

Related Resources

Fiction

Persuasion by Jane Austen
Pride and Prejudice by Jane Austen
Jane Eyre by Charlotte Brontë
Wuthering Heights by Emily Brontë
The Everlasting Covenant by Robyn Carr
An American Tragedy by Theodore Dreiser
Romeo and Juliet by William Shakespeare, retold by Bruce Coville
Shakespeare Made Easy: Romeo and Juliet by William Shakespeare, retold by Alan Durband

Chapter Six

Information for Teachers: Resources and the Law

Before showing any film to your class, be sure to preview it. Descriptions and information obtained from this book, the World Wide Web, and video guides may not be sufficient for you to make judgments about the suitability of the film for your class. While viewing the film you can also make instructional decisions regarding the length of the clips you wish to show at any one time. Your objectives, class time, and interests, as well as the needs of your students, will be the ultimate factors for integrating a particular foreign film with English subtitles into your curriculum.

RESOURCES

All of the films included in this book were obtained free or for a nominal cost through the public library or local video store. A number of catalogs exist for ordering foreign films. The following are two sources listed for your convenience, but finding and ordering a specific film is easily done on the Internet.

1. *Facets Complete Video Catalog*
   www.facets.org
   Includes international cinema
2. MoviesUnlimited.com
   www.moviesunlimited.com
   Includes foreign films

The foreign film guides in chapter 5 provide detailed information to help you choose the best films for your class. You may find extra information about specific films from video guides and the World Wide Web. The following three video guides provide additional useful information:

2003 Movie and Video Guide by Leonard Maltin
The Off-Hollywood Film Guide by Tom Wiener
VideoHound's World Cinema by Elliot Wilhelm

TeachWithMovies.com is an excellent source of information for using movies in the classroom. For a nominal annual subscription rate, you can have access to film guides for a large number of films, including some foreign films with English subtitles.

THE LAW

At the very beginning of each copyrighted film is the directive "For Home Use Only." Like the old "Do not remove under penalty of law" tags that were sewn into pillows, the home use warning for videos has been a cause for consternation. Have teachers who have been showing films in their classrooms been breaking the law? Not likely, though the law varies about the use of films for educational purposes in school classrooms depending on how the film is procured, how it is used, and when it is used.

As teachers, you have a legal responsibility to know and follow the law regarding the use of copyright protected materials in your classroom. Section 110 (1) of Title 17 of the United States Code on Copyright and Conditions cites the following exemption for the use of copyrighted films for educational purposes:

> Performance or display of a work by instructors or pupils in the course of face-to-face teaching activities of a nonprofit educational institution, in a classroom or similar place devoted to instruction, unless in the case of a motion picture or other audiovisual work, the performance, or the display of individual images, is given by means of a copy that was not lawfully made under this title, and that the person responsible for the performance knew or had reason to believe was not lawfully made.

The exemption states that videos and DVDs with U.S. copyrights that have been rented, checked out from a library, or purchased can be used in the classroom for educational, nonprofit purposes provided teachers follow these guidelines:

1. Films must be shown in a classroom or place intended for instruction for nonprofit purposes.
2. Films must be for planned educational purposes, not for extracurricular entertainment.
3. Films must be shown by the teacher to the students in a face-to-face encounter.

The Teach Act passed on November 2, 2002, and signed into law by President George W. Bush has loosened the restrictions on the copyrighted materials, including videos, teachers can use in the classroom (Crews, 2004). Though the act specifically addresses copyright issues confronting online learning, classroom teachers are included under the umbrella of protection. Even with the Teach Act's relaxed requirements, teachers must follow these guidelines:

1. Teachers must not make copies of the film.
2. Teachers must not use the film for public performances.
3. Teachers must not make a profit from the film.

Under no circumstance can teachers legally show a pirated copy of a film. A good rule of thumb for knowing whether an action is illegal is to determine whether the action causes the person holding the copyright to lose money. If the answer is "yes," the action is most likely illegal.

Public television programs are protected by copyright law. Within strict guidelines, the *fair use doctrine* permits the nonprofit use of films taped from a television broadcast without permission from the copyright holder. Handman (1996) explains a set of guidelines developed in 1981 by the Kastenmeir Committee. The 1981 Guidelines for Off-the-Air Recording of Broadcast Programming for Educational Purposes state that teachers can show films taped from a public television broadcast for educational purposes within the following limitations:

1. The taped show must include the copyright notice.
2. The tape may be shown once within 10 days of the taping and one other time for review or reinforcement.
3. The tape may be held for 45 days for evaluation to determine whether it should be purchased. After 45 days, the tape must be destroyed.

Teachers taping television programs delivered by cable or satellite are not covered by the fair use guidelines listed previously because the programs are not free to the public. Teachers are required to check with the station or network before taping a program carried by cable or satellite (Botterbusch, 1996.)

Films rented, checked out from a public library, or purchased are not subject to the same restrictions as films taped from a public broadcast.

Many legitimate sources exist for procuring foreign films for a nominal charge or for free at the public library for classroom use.

As you continue to look for new and innovative ways to engage your students in learning, you will be looking to technology for help. Videos, the Internet, online pen pal organizations, online book clubs, and computer software are just a few of the tools available to meet the needs and interests of students in the 21st century. The law enables nonprofit organizations, including educational facilities, to make extensive use of copyrighted materials without seeking and paying for permission. It is advisable to check your school's policies regarding using copyrighted materials in the classroom. Be sure to check the law frequently for clarification and changes. You can access the United States Copyright Office by going online at www.copyright.gov.

REFERENCES

Botterbusch, H. R. (1996). *Copyright in the age of new technology* (Fastback #405). Bloomington, IN: Phi Delta Kappa.

Crews, K. D. (2004). *New copyright law for distance education: The meaning and importance of the TEACH Act.* American Library Association Fact Sheet Number 7, at www.copyright.iupui.edu (accessed November 17, 2004).

Handman, G. (1996). *Frequently asked film and video copyright questions.* University of California Berkeley Library, at www.lib.berkeley.edu/MRC/Copy right.html (accessed November 17, 2004).

Maltin, L. (2003). *Movie and video guide.* New York: Signet.

United States Copyright Office. (2004). United States Code on Copyright and Conditions, at www.copyright.gov (accessed November 17, 2004).

Wiener, T. (2002). *The off-Hollywood film guide.* New York: Random House.

Wilhelm, E. (1999). *VideoHound's world cinema.* Detroit: Visible Ink Press.

Appendix: List of Films and Awards

1. *The 400 Blows* (1959) French 4 Stars

   Grades 9–12

   A coming-of-age film in which a troubled 13-year-old boy tries to fit into a society fraught with social ills. Social and family issues are the underlying themes of this movie.

   Awards:
   1960 Academy Awards, nominated for Best Writing, Story, and Screenplay
   1960 Bodil Award, Best European Film
   1960 French Syndicate of Cinema Critics, Best Film
   1959 Cannes Film Festival, Best Director
   1959 New York Film Critics Circle Award, Best Foreign Language Film

2. *Au Revoir, les Enfants* (1987) French 3½ Stars

   Grades 9–12

   During World War II, three Jewish boys hide from the evils of Nazi Germany in a Catholic boarding school. Though ever fearful of being found, they exhibit typical preadolescent behaviors, including a longing to fit in with their peers and an awakening interest in girls.

   Awards:
   1989 BAFTA Award, Best Director
   1989 Bodil Award, Best European Film

1989 César Award, Best Director
1988 Academy Awards, nominated for Best Script and Best Foreign Language Film
1987 Venice Film Festival, Best Director

3. *Babette's Feast* (1987) Danish, French 4 Stars
Grades 9–12

This story of two young women in a tiny Danish town spans a time period of 50 years. Entertaining and thought provoking, this film shows how the culture of the town is influenced by people from outside the community. Time, continuity, and change are integral parts of this film.

Awards:
1989 BAFTA Award, Best Film Not in the English Language
1989 London Film Critics Circle Award, Actor of the Year (Stéphane Audran) and Foreign Language Film of the Year
1988 Academy Award, Best Foreign Language Film
1987 Cannes Film Festival, Prize of the Ecumenical Jury, accepted by Gabriel Axel

4. *Beauty and the Beast* (1946) French 4 Stars
Grades 6–12

To save his own life, a father sends his beautiful daughter to live with the Beast. Though initially frightened and repulsed, the beautiful daughter looks at the kind soul of the Beast and falls in love. A story of betrayal, jealousy, acceptance, and love that shows human behavior at its best and its worst.

5. *The Bicycle Thief* (1948) Italian 4 Stars
Grades 6–12

In post–World War II Italy, jobs are scarce and citizens are forced to sell household goods to buy food. A story of a father who is forced to make a choice between honesty and survival. The relationship between father and son at the end of the film is tragically altered. Civic ideals are questioned and challenged in this film.

Awards:
1951 Bodil Award, Best European Film
1950 Honorary Academy Award, Outstanding Foreign Language Film (a special Academy Award for foreign films before foreign films had a category of their own)
1950 BAFTA Award, Best Film from Any Source
1950 Golden Globe Award, Best Foreign Film
1949 Italian National Syndicate of Film Journalists, Silver Ribbon for Best Score
1949 New York Film Critics Circle Award, Best Foreign Language Film

6. *Children of Heaven* (1997) Persian 3 Stars
Grades 6–12
A poignant story about family life in modern-day Iran. Two children share a secret about a lost pair of shoes that would put stress on their family and get them into trouble. The children seek ways to avoid revealing their secret to their parents, schoolmaster, and members of the community while seeking a solution to their problem. This film provides insights into the universal feelings and needs of people.

Awards:
1999 Academy Awards, nominated for Best Foreign Language Film
1998 Newport International Film Festival, Best Foreign Film
1997 Fajr Film Festival, Best Film
1997 Montréal World Film Festival, Best Director
1997 Oulu International Children's Film Festival, Best Foreign Film

7. *Crouching Tiger, Hidden Dragon* (2000) Mandarin 2½ Stars
Grades 9–12
A martial arts film set in 19th-century China. Along with plenty of action, two love stories are intertwined, tied together by a stolen sword. Chinese family values and traditions are challenged by a woman who does not want to marry and instead would rather be a warrior. Feminism, exhibited by the heroine, occurs at a time of a male-dominated culture, making it nearly impossible to think and act as an

independent woman. An underlying theme of being true to oneself provides opportunities to set personal expectations and goals.

Awards:
2002 Grammy Award, Best Soundtrack Album for a Motion Picture, Television, or other Visual Media
2001 Academy Award, Best Foreign Language Film, Best Art Direction, Best Cinematography, and Best Original Score
2001 BAFTA Award, Best Film Not in the English Language
2001 Bodil Award, Best Non-American Film
2001 Golden Globe Award, Best Director and Best Foreign Language Film
2001 Hong Kong Film Award, Best Action Choreography, Best Cinematography, Best Director, Best Original Film Score, Best Original Film Song, Best Picture, Best Sound Design, and Best Supporting Actress (Pei-pei Cheng)

8. *The Cup* (1999) Bhutanese 3 Stars
Grades 6–12

A story about the traditions of the past upheld by the older monks and the dream and determination of a spirited student monk to bring television to the monastery. The student monk wants to see the 1998 World Cup football (soccer) games. Young student monks living a life of sacrifice in a third-world country demonstrate interests and emotions of young boys everywhere.

Awards:
2000 Kerala International Film Festival, Special Jury Prize for "its freshness of touch and vivid representation of a spiritual (and very human) world which cinema had left so far unexplored."
1999 Amiens International Film Festival, Special Jury Award
1999 Munich Film Festival, Best Director
1999 Pusan International Film Festival, Best Director "for an irreverently humorous and still respectful portrayal of a Buddhist community, presenting a simple story in an arresting manner while avoiding the usual tools of commercial filmmaking."

9. *Day of Wrath* (1943) Danish 3½ Stars

Grades 9–12

The most famous witchcraft trials were held in Salem, Massachusetts, in 1692. This film is a story about a 1623 equivalent in Denmark. The film's approach to witchcraft is not general outrage but how one clergyman deals with his guilt and anguish after exonerating a woman, accused of witchcraft, solely in order to marry her young daughter. The resulting family dynamic provides a focus on the connection of past events to the future.

10. *East/West* (1999) French, Russian 2 Stars

Grades 9–12

A tragic and historical tale about Russian expatriates who, with great expectations and patriotism, return to the aid of their motherland in the aftermath of World War II. The film follows the plight of a doctor and his family from the time they board the ship taking them from France to Russia, throughout the years they spend coping with the institution of communism, to their eventual plot to escape the deceit and tyranny of the Russian government. Differences between French and Soviet Union governments provide a clear contrast for reflection and study.

Awards:
2000 Miami Film Festival, Best Director
2000 Palm Springs International Film Festival, Best Director
2000 Santa Barbara International Film Festival, Best Director
1999 National Board of Review, Best Foreign Film

11. *Grand Illusion* (1937) French, German 4 Stars

Grades 9–12

The story takes place in a German prison camp during World War I. French prisoners of war and their German captors are, of course, distinguished by their nationalities. However, issues evolving from social class take precedence over differences in nationality. In a time of war, are class differences relevant, or are differences between people just an illusion? This question can be extended to class differences and human behavior in our lives today.

Awards:
1939 Academy Awards, nominated for Best Picture
1939 New York Film Critics Circle Award, Best Foreign Language Film
1938 National Board of Review, Best Foreign Film
1937 Venice Film Festival, Best Director

12. *The Hidden Fortress* (1958) Japanese 3½ Stars
Grades 9–12
This film was the inspiration for George Lucas's *Star Wars*.
In the aftermath of a war between two warlords, two comedic, bumbling characters trying to return to their home meet a John Wayne–type stranger. One narrow escape follows another in this comedy set in Japan in the 16th century. This film shows life without modern technology and conveniences. The characters make do with primitive transportation, few creature comforts, and, except for gunpowder, rather crude weaponry.

Awards:
1959 Berlin International Film Festival, Best Director
1959 Blue Ribbon Award, Best Film
1958 Kinema Junpo Award, Best Screenplay

13. *Jean de Florette* (1986) French 3½ Stars
Grades 6–12
A tragic tale set in France shortly after World War I about an inexperienced farmer and the greedy neighbors who want his land. The farmer, who toils in spite of a physical handicap, has exceptional success growing crops and livestock until faced with a drought. His neighbors and members of the community harbor a secret that could save the farmer's crops and livestock. This duplicity, motivated by greed, illustrates the power that natural resources and the interdependence of people within a community have on a single individual.

Awards:
1988 BAFTA Award, Best Actor in a Supporting Role (Daniel Auteuil), Best Adapted Screenplay, Best Cinematography, and Best Film
1988 London Film Critics Circle Award, Best Foreign Language Film of the Year
1987 César Award, Best Actor (Daniel Auteuil)
1987 National Board of Review, Best Foreign Language Film
1986 National Academy of Cinema, Best Director

14. *Life Is Beautiful* (1997) Italian, German 3½ Stars
Grades 6–12
When a father is faced with the responsibility for the survival of his young son in a German concentration camp, he resorts to humor and storytelling to keep him safe from the German guards. The story is, at once, uplifting, humorous, and tragic. Endurance, self-determination, sacrifice, and problem solving are some of the human elements portrayed in this film.

Awards:
1999 Academy Award, Best Actor (Roberto Benigni), Best Score, and Best Foreign Language Film
1999 BAFTA Award, Best Performance by an Actor in a Leading Role (Roberto Benigni)
1999 César Award, Best Foreign Film
1998 AFI Fest, Best Feature Film
1998 Cannes Film Festival, Best Actor (Roberto Benigni)
1998 National Board of Review, Special Achievement in Filmmaking

15. *M* (1931) German 4 Stars
Grades 9–12
A thoughtful portrayal of justice and group dynamics. A tragic story about a serial child killer in Berlin is portrayed without explicit violence; crimes are committed off screen. The story relies on foreshadowing and symbols such as a lost balloon to lead viewers to make inferences about the killer.

16. *The Mystery of Kaspar Hauser* (1975) German 3½ Stars
Grades 9–12

After spending the first 16 years of his life in a cellar, Kaspar Hauser is introduced to civilization in Germany in 1826. The townsfolk take care of him, introduce him to language, and teach him skills to fit into society. The juxtaposition of civilized social traditions and the simplistic traits and views of the world stemming from Kaspar's wild nature create interesting incidents that generate ideas and questions about nurture and nature.

Awards:
1975 Cannes Film Festival, Best Director
1975 German Film Award, Outstanding Individual Achievement: Editing and Outstanding Individual Achievement: Production Design

17. *Rashomon* (1950) Japanese 4 Stars
Grades 9–12
The Outrage, an American version of *Rashomon*, was made in 1964.
This famous Japanese film shows four different versions of the same crime as told by eyewitnesses. The versions are radically different and call into question our ability to relate honestly the reality of traumatic events. This film moves beyond simple point of view to an underlying human trait of preserving one's reputation through the selective recounting of events.

Awards:
1953 Academy Awards, nominated for Best Art Direction
1951 Blue Ribbon Award, Best Screenplay
1951 National Board of Review, Best Director
1951 Venice Film Festival, Best Director
1950 Mainichi Film Concours, Best Actress (Machiko Kyô)

18. *Seven Samurai* (1954) Japanese 4 Stars
Grades 6–12
The Magnificent Seven is a remake of this film.
When a small Japanese village is plundered by bandits, the village people immediately give up all hope for a future. A few natural leaders emerge during this time of loss and grief. The leaders search for

seven hungry samurai willing to help defend their village for food. This film illustrates important concepts of working together to solve problems, detailed planning, and responsibility to oneself, family, and neighbors.

Awards:
1957 Academy Awards, nominated for Best Art Direction and Best Costume Design
1954 Mainichi Film Concours, Best Supporting Actor (Seiji Miyaguchi)
1954 Venice Film Festival, Best Director

19. *Umbrellas of Cherbourg* (1964) French 3½ Stars
Grades 9–12
This musical drama, where all the dialogue is sung, takes place in Cherbourg, France, during the 1950s. The story is about a young girl and her first love. The young lovers can't escape choices that come with the grown-up responsibilities of life. Obligations to family members, young and old, stimulate interesting practical and moral questions.

Awards:
1966 Academy Awards, nominated for Best Music and Best Writing, Story, and Screenplay
1965 French Syndicate of Cinema Critics, Best Film
1964 Cannes Film Festival, Best Director

20–23. *War and Peace*, Parts I–IV (1968) Russian, French 4 Stars
Grades 9–12
Based on Leo Tolstoy's novel, this film centers on the Napoleonic invasion of Eastern Europe from 1805 to 1812. The musical score, photography of the Russian countryside, magnificent ballrooms, and battle scenes attract and hold the viewers' attention. Some universal truths emerge from this film. For example, there are only two harms in life: illnesses and remorse. Prince Andrei, a Russian army officer, notes another when he likens his own life to an oak tree, barren for a

season, but with time and endurance, it changes to become productive and lush.

Awards:
1969 Academy Award, Best Foreign Language Film
1969 Golden Globe Award, Best Foreign Language Film
1968 New York Film Critics Circle Award, Best Foreign Language Film

24. *Wuthering Heights* (1954) Spanish 1½ Stars
Grades 9–12
A Spanish remake of Emily Brontë's novel about love twisted by fanaticism. Catalina, comfortably married to Eduardo, meets up with her one true love, Alejandro. Their passion makes it impossible for them to ignore their feelings for one another. In the end, death brings them together.

REFERENCES

Maltin, L. (2003). *Movie and video guide.* New York: Signet

WEBSITES

www.foreignfilms.com
www.IMBD.com

Index